INFINITE YOU

Also by Pamala Oslie:

BOOKS

Life Colors: What the Colors in Your Aura Reveal

Make Your Dreams Come True: Simple Steps for Changing the Beliefs That Limit You

Love Colors: A New Approach to Love, Relationships, and Auras

GUIDED IMAGERY MEDITATIONS (AUDIO)

Abundance

Attracting Love: A Fabulous Woman

Attracting Love: A Wonderful Man

Relaxation & Health

WORKSHOPS (AUDIO)

Infinite You Workshop

Live An Amazing Life! Being Your True Self

Life Colors: What Your Aura Colors Say About You

Developing Your Intuitive and Psychic Abilities

Available at www.LifeColorsCity.com

INFINITE YOU

Discover Your Quantum Powers, Parallel Universes,

Telepathy, Spirituality, and More

Pamala Oslie

OSLIE PRESS
SANTA BARBARA, CALIFORNIA

Pamala Oslie is not a doctor, professional health care practitioner, or licensed therapist. Her information, advice, and suggestions are not intended to replace professional guidance from your licensed practitioners. Please seek professional advice from your medical doctors, health care practitioners, and licensed therapists.

Every effort has been made to ensure that the websites mentioned in this book are accurate as of the time of original publication. However, neither the publisher nor the author can guarantee their continued existence or accuracy.

OSLIE PRESS
Website: www.AuraColors.com

Editing: Stephanie Gunning
Cover designer: Pro_ebook Covers
Interior design: Gus Yoo

978-0-9849375-9-2 (paperback)
978-0-9849375-2-3 (ebook)

To Life,
in all of its beautiful expressions

Contents

❧

Introduction

"Reality is merely an illusion, albeit a very persistent one."
—ALBERT EINSTEIN (1879–1955), NOBEL PRIZE-WINNING PHYSICIST

Imagine for a moment that you are a one-dimensional being living in a one-dimensional world. This means you are just a point on a line. You can only move back and forth on a straight line, and you don't perceive anything outside of your one-dimensional existence.

Now imagine you are a two-dimensional being living in a two-dimensional world. You are now a flat dot on a flat piece of paper. In this two-dimensional world, you are able to move back and forth, side to side, and around in circles on the flat piece of paper. You have more freedom than a one-dimensional being, which is more fun . . . but still you can only go back and forth, side to side, and around in circles on a flat piece of paper.

Suppose that one day one of the two-dimensional dots gets bored with just moving back and forth and side to side on this one piece of paper. He senses there is more to life, so he gathers up his courage and decides to take a risk. He pauses . . . wonders whether or not what he's about to do is even possible . . . and suddenly leaps up above the flat piece of paper. Then he falls back down. Excitedly, he does it again. Then he does it once more.

Filled with joy, the dot rushes over to the other dots and shares his incredible news. "There's more! We aren't stuck to this one piece of paper. We're not limited to back and forth and side to side," he says. "I've seen more. We can go up and down! There's another dimension!"

The other two-dimensional beings ignore him and go about their business of moving back and forth, side to side, and around in circles. Although the excited dot tells them again and again how they are not limited to a simple existence on a flat piece of paper and that they can have a fuller life, the other dots don't understand what he's saying. They don't understand the concept of "up and down." It's not part of their reality. They have never heard of such a thing, nor have they ever experienced it. And truthfully, they aren't really interested in knowing about it: Going up and down sounds strange and too complicated. Plus, they are too busy moving back and forth on the piece of paper. Everything they know exists in their flat, two-dimensional world.

But the dot doesn't give up. He wants others to have the same experience and taste the same freedom so he continues to share his story. Some of the dots finally become so irritated by him that they declare him a delusional troublemaker and send him off to the far side of the paper, hoping he will no longer be a bother.

A few of the other dots, however, become curious. They too have grown restless and dissatisfied with their limitations; they sense that possibly there is more to existence. Soon another two-dimensional dot decides to take a risk. She pauses for a moment and then leaps up and off the paper. Then another dot leaps . . . and another. The first dot was right, there *is* another dimension, and there is more to life! They can now leap up and down. They excitedly rush to share their experiences with the others. But the other two-dimensional dots still refuse to listen as they continue on with their lives.

One day, as the first dot leaps up off the paper, he pauses for a moment and looks down. He realizes he's not just jumping up and down, he *is* up and down. He has height! He has height and depth and an inside and an outside. He's not just a flat two-dimensional being. He's not just a dot on a piece of paper jumping into a three-dimensional world. He is a three-dimensional *being* that exists in a three-dimensional world. He realizes that he had always been that and he had only been experiencing a portion of who he truly was. He now had a whole new world to explore as a liberated three-dimensional being.

TODAY, WE PERCEIVE OURSELVES AS THREE-DIMENSIONAL BEINGS. We've been taught that reality is three-dimensional—and in fact, this fits with what our physical senses tell us so usually we have no reason to question it. Everything we see in our world appears three-dimensional: with height, width, and depth. We can move back and forth, side to side, up and down, in and out. But . . . are we actually more than this? Do we have a limited perception of reality?

The astonishing truth is that you are not just a three-dimensional being. You are an infinite and multidimensional being!

You are far grander than you realize. Being an infinite being doesn't just mean you will have greater freedom and enhanced abilities once you escape your *physical* body at the end of your life. You are an unlimited being now, someone with amazing abilities that extend beyond the known, but limited three dimensions we are so familiar with. These inherent skills exceed what most people believe is possible, and some would say they are *impossible*. Many of us are living proof, however, that these abilities are real. Like the first few dots to jump off of the paper, we've already been experiencing life beyond the accepted three-dimensional boundaries. And if some of us have these expansive talents, *everyone* has them.

Albert Einstein introduced the *special theory of relativity*, which led to the conclusion that the fabric of spacetime is a component of the fourth dimension.[1] All of us do experience time. However, we only experience some of the fourth dimension. Based on appearances, we might think time only moves forward. But interestingly, some physicists have theorized that time may also go backward *and sideways*.[2] *And some theorize that time doesn't exist at all*.[3] But we don't *appear* to live that way . . . yet.

I believe we are evolving into a more highly developed species, one with a superior level of awareness and greater abilities. Or it may be that we are finally *waking up* to our true nature and realizing that we are exceptional beings. We've lived too long thinking we're just little pawns on the chessboard—and acting as if we have little or no power. It's time to see that we are much more. Because so many people have been demonstrating unusual and advanced abilities, it's time to reassess our definition of *human being* and live our greater potential here and now.

A SPECIAL NOTE TO YOU

My sincere desire is to know that you are happy, healthy, filled with love and joy, and living your greatest dreams. I believe that we are experiencing a positive shift on the planet. Many people claim that we are in the midst of a consciousness evolution and I agree with them. I am witnessing it firsthand. I see more and more people embracing spiritual and metaphysical concepts, wanting to learn about natural and holistic ways to heal, showing an interest in advanced abilities, and demonstrating many unusual skills.

I honor your chosen beliefs and personal life path, just as I honor every person's choices. I absolutely believe in free will. I know that you have a specific purpose for being on the planet. I acknowledge that everyone has different beliefs, perspectives, and experiences; no two people anywhere in the world share the exact same ideas about life. So I am not sharing the information in this book to challenge your chosen life direction or your philosophical, moral, ethical, religious, or spiritual beliefs. If what you believe brings you a sense of inner peace and contentment, your beliefs are obviously aligned with your true self. I trust that you will follow your own inner guidance and sense of truth as I share my information and experiences with you.

My goal in writing *Infinite You* is to *enhance* your life experiences and to add more joy and enrichment to the world by sharing news of what is possible for all of us. I choose to believe in love-based principles and empowering beliefs that can help us experience more trust, self-sovereignty, and fulfillment. After decades of living with enhanced abilities, exploring spiritual principles, and delving into quantum physics, I've discovered that there is more to reality and who we are. I've also experienced much more freedom, love, and joy in my life because I've developed these advanced abilities. So I'm sharing this information with you in the hope that it will inspire you to leap off the page and live a more amazing life.

CHAPTER ONE

YOU ARE GREATER

*"The day science begins to study non-physical phenomena,
it will make more progress in one decade than it has
in all the previous centuries of its existence."*
—NIKOLA TESLA (1856–1943), FUTURIST, INVENTOR, ENGINEER

As babies, when we had developed enough to become
mobile, we began crawling. Soon after, something inside
us urged us to stand upright and walk. Why would we go
from the stability of hands and knees, firmly supported on the
ground, to balancing precariously on wobbly legs and two tiny
feet? Intuitively we must have known that it was time for more:
We sensed that walking would ultimately give us more freedom,
more fulfillment, and greater experiences than crawling. We
somehow knew that walking would improve and expand our lives.

Actually, all our advances seem to have the same goal: more
freedom, more ease, and more fulfilling experiences. But are we
done evolving? Have we reached the pinnacle of our potential?

Once again, we appear to be transforming. Just as the ability
to stand and walk was always within us, and we eventually reached
the stage when it was time for that ability to surface, our greater
selves are now emerging. Just like the oak tree is contained

within the acorn and it slowly emerges to live its full grandness, so too are we transforming and allowing a more expansive self to appear. Many people aren't aware that there is something profound happening with humankind. However, many others have sensed that it's time to evolve and go beyond our currently accepted limitations. In addition, along with this inner evolution, very significant information is being revealed in science that could ultimately have a powerful and positive impact on our lives as well.

My Story: An Example That Reveals That a New Consciousness Is Emerging

One evening in the 1980s, I began my adventures into expanded consciousness. No, drugs were not involved. I was at an event to hear the late English shaman Reverend Michael Bromley speak. I was stunned when he pulled me up in front of the group and told me I had special abilities. He informed me that I had been asking to go to the next level in my life (he was right) and said it was now time to develop my skills. He threw me in the proverbial "deep end" and instructed me to start sharing the intuitive information I was sensing about people.

That evening I was shocked to discover that I did know accurate and very detailed information about complete strangers. When I focused my attention on different people in the room, I would sense a connection with them. Feelings or images would emerge in my awareness. I would suddenly feel sad or lonely when I focused on someone and I knew those weren't my own personal feelings. Other times, a picture or short movie would appear in my inner vision and I sensed I was watching something about a person's life. Sometimes thoughts would pop into my mind, as if people were telepathically sharing information about their lives with me. Each time I focused on someone specific, I experienced a subtle knowingness about him or her. I felt compassion for everyone I focused on, as if I had known each my entire life.

I knew a woman in the room was pregnant because in my inner vision (in my mind) I saw the spirit of a little girl standing next to her. The woman didn't know she was pregnant. Days later, I heard through a mutual friend that the woman went to her doctor and found out she was in fact pregnant; and months later she did have a baby girl.

When I turned my attention to another woman in the room, I had a vision of her being frustrated and struggling with an old green car. She verified that she had borrowed a neighbor's dilapidated green car to come to that evening's event because her car wouldn't start. She had been stressed and upset because she couldn't figure out how to operate that car.

It was an interesting evening of *seeing* one detailed vision after another, each proving to be accurate. That night, I discovered I had a sixth sense. I was psychic and telepathic!

The next few months were like a whirlwind as I uncovered more and more remarkable abilities. During those months, I opened up my ability to see energy fields (auras), and today I know important information about people based on the colors in their auras. Also, I discovered how to intentionally use energy, thoughts, and feelings to create my heart's desires.

A short time later, I learned of the existence of parallel universes and discovered that I could deliberately move in and out of them to change my life. Also I developed my ability to talk to people who have crossed over—meaning, those who have died. In addition, I realized I was able to see people's other lives (often referred to as past lives). It has been a remarkable journey.

The most important point to all of this is that if I have these amazing abilities it means we *all* do! These are natural skills that every human being has. Most people just aren't aware of it yet.

WHY SHOULD WE BE INTERESTED IN THIS?

Developing any of these abilities can dramatically improve the quality of your life. On a personal level, it can make you more insightful, compassionate, and empowered, and better able to trust yourself. Globally, it can improve our relations with one another and help us create better, life-enhancing solutions for the world. To paraphrase Albert Einstein, we cannot solve a problem from the same level of thinking, with the same mind, that created the problem in the first place. He also said, "A new type of thinking is essential if mankind is to survive and move toward higher levels."[1]

So according to Einstein, in order to change our lives and our world, we *need* to change our thinking. Our understanding of who we are, our capabilities, how we interact with each other, and what we can accomplish have to evolve.

To help us with this shift in our thinking, quantum physicists also have important information to contribute to the process. Quantum physics is the study of particles at the smallest levels, the subatomic levels. These physicists are revealing new, life-altering concepts and reexamining *everything* we've believed about reality. They have evidence that reality is not what we believe it is! They have made remarkable discoveries that could radically change our lives—forever.

Unfortunately, most of us are not living this new model or acting on this advanced knowledge yet. We haven't been taught these new possibilities. Most people are still living with old ideas about the world, as if nothing profound is occurring.

Imagine that experts inform you aerodynamics is a natural law and therefore flight is possible. You discover that you could fly across the country in a matter of hours. You thank the experts, but travel across the country in a horse-drawn covered wagon instead. We're doing something similar today: We're not taking advantage of the newest findings. Our limited understanding of reality has been preventing us from living our greatest potential. For that reason, we'll be exploring some of these remarkable discoveries to help us understand what is truly possible.

These exciting and powerful discoveries will make life easier, provide more freedom, and appear just as magical as flying across the country would have seemed to those who lived centuries ago. Quantum physics has already altered our lives by giving us most of our new technologies (personal computers, smartphones, iPods, and more)[2], but now it's time to see what it reveals about us.

If enough of us were to courageously step beyond our familiar boundaries, embrace this new information about the nature of reality, and fully activate our own advanced capabilities, we would open the way for others to do the same, which could lead to a vastly different understanding of the world and an entirely new way of life. This is the way transformation has happened throughout history: brave explorers and mavericks are always the ones who break through old thinking and reveal what's possible for the rest. Are you ready to metaphorically leap up off the page now, too?

CHAPTER TWO

YOUR NATURAL ABILITIES

"The only way of discovering the limits of the possible is to venture a little way past them into the impossible."
—SIR ARTHUR C. CLARKE (1917–2008), FUTURIST, SCIENCE FICTION AUTHOR, INVENTOR

Some might call the following talents *gifts*. For myself, I consider *life* to be a gift and view these abilities as natural and inherent in each of us. You can activate any of these abilities at any time. Some people may be more proficient with some of these skills, just as some are more adept at being musicians, singers, or athletes. But all of us have the capacity to learn each one. If we all support one another in developing these advanced, but natural skills, we can create a better life for everyone.

YOUR ABILITIES

What are your natural abilities and why are they important? Among other things:

- You have the ability to use thought and energy to affect physical objects, manifest your desires, heal your body, influence the weather, and more.

- You have intuitive, telepathic, and psychic abilities. You can see outside of time and space to know the past, present, and future.

- You can sense energy fields, or auras, and know significant information about people based on the frequencies or colors in their energy fields.

- You can intentionally move into parallel universes to change your life.

- You can see other lives, also called "past" lives by some.

- You can talk to people who have died and crossed over to the other side.

Because there are thousands of people stepping forward now with these same unusual abilities, we can no longer ignore them or declare them flukes and aberrations. If even one person can demonstrate these advanced skills, don't we have a responsibility, an obligation, to see what is going on? Isn't it possible that humanity could benefit by exploring these abilities more closely and discovering what is truly possible?

The fact that many of us experience these abilities proves that there is more to us than we've been taught, and the fact that many of us use these skills to benefit others as well as ourselves shows there are good reasons to develop them.

THE BENEFITS OF DEVELOPING THESE ABILITIES

Why is it a good idea to explore our potential and develop these superior skills?

If we have these valuable talents and we don't develop them, we are like birds trapped in a cage whose beautiful wings are useless. We yearn for a better life, all the while ignoring what we are fully capable of accomplishing. Now we have the keys to move beyond the cage and create a more wondrous life for ourselves. These abilities can help us:

- **Change our lives.** We can use them to go beyond our perceived limitations and become happier, more loving, and more empowered beings. We have limited our self-expression and life experiences by believing we are incapable or helpless. We are capable of more.

- Make life easier. Once we understand how the universe really works and learn about the true principles of creation, we can design our lives and create with little or no effort.

- **Reduce fear and eventually stop pain and suffering altogether.** Once we tap into our deeper guidance and use these abilities, we can become more trusting, self-confident, and joyful. Once fear melts away, hopelessness and suffering can also dissolve.

- **Create more compassion, love, and understanding in the world.** Once we understand and experience our connection, we will know that there is no need to judge anyone, including ourselves, and love and acceptance can flow more freely.

- **Improve our health and wellbeing.** Once we trust our true connection with life, once we tap into our inner guidance and learn to follow it, fear and stress diminish. Living stress-free lives can prevent illnesses and accidents.

- **Improve the world and live with global abundance rather than hunger, poverty, and scarcity.** Once we understand the natural, creative principles of the universe, we can create with a sense of inner power and infinite possibilities rather than constrict in fear and limited thinking.

- **Create with unbounded freedom and joy.**

Cultivating these abilities often generates deeper love, a stronger sense of connection, greater trust and inner peace. I know that has been my experience. Other people have reported similar feelings.

As we went from crawling to walking to riding bicycles to driving cars to flying planes, each method gave us more freedom. Developing these enhanced abilities promises to do the same. However, just as some people will never choose to learn to drive a car and most will never learn to pilot a plane, even though developing those skills could result in having more freedom, no one *needs* to learn any of these expanded abilities. You can always choose the abilities that interest you and ignore the others. This information is being offered as an alternative to our old and restrictive thinking. Being able to activate these abilities is an option few people know they have.

MAGIC

Some may claim that the abilities we discuss in this book sound like "magical thinking." Based on our current understanding of *reality* and our definition of *human,* these abilities can certainly seem magical. But many things once classified as magic are now considered commonplace and real.

So first, let's define the term magic. According to Merriam-Webster.com, it is:

An extraordinary power or influence, seemingly from a supernatural source.

The only reason people may think these powers are supernatural is that they haven't understood them or used them—until now.

Many ideas throughout history were judged to be magical thinking or fantasy until we understood the natural principles behind them. For example, going to the moon was once thought to be unrealistic, something that was relegated to science fiction novels, until we understood the natural laws that could make that real. Then science fiction became science fact.

Many items that we accept as normal today would have been considered magical thinking or science fiction centuries ago, or even a few decades ago: smartphones, computers, television, satellites, and the list continues. So what are we disregarding today because it seems unrealistic or too fantastic to believe?

You may doubt that *you* have these "magical" capabilities. But the abilities we'll be discussing are *natural* aspects of the human experience, as so many people are now proving, which means that you do have them. As a child, you may have known you had these special skills, but then you were taught to stop believing in them. Do you remember enjoying stories of fairy godmothers, magic wands, the flying Peter Pan, or the wizardly Harry Potter? The reason these stories are so popular is because there's something inside us that resonates with them. We sense—not just wish—that the *magical* abilities these characters demonstrate are real and part of our true nature.

To show you there is logic and science behind these skills, and to show you this book is not just based on *"woo-woo"* thinking, in the chapters that follow we'll discuss the physics and the technology that supports their existence. Understanding some of the basic scientific principles may help you trust they are, in fact, real and make you better able to develop your own abilities.

"When a distinguished but elderly scientist states that something is possible, he is almost certainly right. When he states that something is impossible, he is very probably wrong."[1]
—ARTHUR C. CLARKE

There will always be those who cling adamantly and defiantly to old paradigms and traditional belief systems. However, there are also those who sense something significant is emerging, something life changing is happening.

While some physicists want to dismiss these extraordinary abilities as unimportant anomalies or label them as *delusions,* other physicists are looking into these capabilities more seriously. These physicists know historically how often accepted scientific "facts" have eventually been proven wrong, and they are therefore more willing to research these previously discounted areas attributed to consciousness. They know quantum physics offers radically different and counterintuitive information about the nature of reality.

"The transition from classical to quantum physics marks a genuine revolution in our understanding of the physical world."[2]
—STANFORD ENCYCLOPEDIA OF PHILOSOPHY

That is a profound statement. Physicists continue to question what we've believed about reality. Beginning to implement what these physicists have been uncovering can change everything.

If you're ready to develop more of your potential, we'll look closely at these abilities, explore why they could be helpful, look at the science behind them, and discuss how you can develop them to improve your own life and the lives of others. Since many people learn best by example, I will also share some of my own personal experiences to show how these skills are possible and are available to you.

CHAPTER THREE

CREATING FROM ENERGY

❧

"You create the world that you know. You have been given perhaps the most awesome gift of all: the ability to project your thoughts outward into physical form."

—JANE ROBERTS, *SETH SPEAKS*

To state it simply and boldly, you can use thought and pure energy to influence matter, create the things that you want, heal your body, influence the weather, and more. In this chapter, I will share my experiences and some different exercises to help you develop your own abilities. Maybe the same or similar techniques will work for you. And then in order to fully comprehend how this is all possible, we'll explore some of the scientific principles, especially those that reveal everything is energy. Understanding that everything is made of energy is paramount to being able to perform all of the following skills.

AFFECTING MATTER

A basic example of how the power of thought can affect matter is the ability to bend spoons. My first experience with this ability was in a class at the International Association on New Science.[1] The instructor was an aerospace engineer. He taught us about the nature of *matter*: that everything is energy, nothing is actually solid, and therefore "matter" is pliable and subject to our thoughts or commands.

Some people have learned to fear their own power, so the thought of *commanding* anything brings up fear that they could abuse or misuse power. Certainly we've seen enough movies that tout the horrors of abusing power to make us fear that possibility. But once you know how truly loving and magnificent you are, you will no longer fear your own power. Until then, if *commanding* is too strong a word, then politely ask something to take a certain form for you. You can use the following example to experiment with this ability yourself.

In the class I attended, we were told to hold a spoon. We were to focus on the spoon and ask it to bend, while we imagined it gently folding over. We focused on bending our spoons for 10–15 minutes, but nothing was happening. Suddenly a woman in the back of the room yelled excitedly. We turned to see her spoon slowly folding over. As soon as we saw that, my spoon and many other people's spoons bent over, too. Apparently seeing that it was possible shifted our beliefs, which allowed our spoons to bend. Unfortunately, the maxim "I'll believe it when I see it" was holding true for some of us.

I've noticed this phenomenon before. People tend to be more successful with a particular ability when they see others doing it. When they see proof that it's possible, it helps them believe.

In my second attempt, I gently held a spoon by two fingers at the very tip of the bowl and two fingers at the bottom tip of the handle. We were told to imagine the spoon becoming liquid. I became quiet and envisioned that in my mind. Within moments, I actually felt it turn into a gel-like liquid and quickly bent the bowl of this previously very rigid, sterling silver spoon.

The instant I realized I was damaging the spoon, it froze in my hands. This was one of strangest sensations I've ever experienced. One minute the item was solid, then it was a gel-like liquid, then it was a twisted solid—right in my hand. This experience once again proved to me that *physical* reality is not what we believe it is.

I bent three more spoons after that and I haven't done so since. I sense that's because I've been taught not to damage or destroy things and this belief is deeply ingrained in my subconscious. I seem to be better at affecting matter when I'm creating something positive rather than damaging something. Many of my students have been able to bend spoons, however. This phenomenon deserves to be researched since we ordinary laypeople are able to achieve something that is supposedly scientifically impossible— at least according to the classical model of physics. It wasn't a "trick." We didn't repeatedly rub the handle until it got hot enough to bend, nor did we forcefully bend the spoon back and forth to weaken the handle, as some skeptics claim. The spoon actually became a thick liquid in my hands, which allowed me to change its form.

Since there isn't much value in owning bent spoons, the point of this exercise is to reveal that consciousness can affect matter. But what if you were to use this knowledge on something else that actually mattered to you? For example, what if you were able to change your body? Since it's made of energy that should work. Would that mean no more stressful dieting?

You have the ability to change the shape and form of your body once you truly realize the power of your thoughts and imagination. No more worrying about what you eat, since everything, including food, is made of energy. It's more important what you believe about your food than what you're actually eating. But you have to really *know* that everything is energy for this to be an effective way for you to change your body.

Or maybe the next time you find yourself cursing your wrinkles as you apply anti-aging face cream, you could imagine instead that all the cells in your body are made of light, then see them glowing with vitality. Feel your whole body glow with light. Continue this experiment for several days or weeks in a row and see if people perceive you as younger and more vibrant.

Or what about creating money from energy?

CREATING MONEY

Often we block prosperity from our lives because we believe in scarcity. We're taught there are a limited number of pieces to the pie and if we get more, others will have less. But everything is energy and the universe is infinitely abundant with energy, so there are no real limits to what can be created.

All the exercises or visualizations I offer are to help you stimulate your imagination and shift your thinking. They're to get you out of old, stuck ways of looking at life. If you can expand your mind and be playful, you can change your thoughts and therefore your experiences. What we believe and imagine will become so.

Here is a fun visualization for manifesting abundance. Imagine money floating down from the sky and landing in big piles all around you. See money in any denomination you want forming out of pure energy and falling from the sky. Every element in the natural world is at its core composed of subatomic particles and space, which are ultimately composed of pure energy. So just envision this energy taking the form of money. Then, see it flowing down around you. This way, you're not using your thoughts against you by imagining you have to work hard for money or that you are taking it away from someone else; you're creating this money out of pure energy.

Every time I do this exercise, cash or something similar shows up in my life. One remarkable example of this occurred a few years ago. A man who I'd never met read one of my books and enjoyed it so much he sent me 100,000 shares of his new company. Those shares ended up being worth $10,000 dollars. This generous gift came to me from a complete stranger right after I did this visualization exercise.

A couple decided to experiment with this same visualization. Every night for five minutes, the couple playfully imagined money floating down from the sky and landing in huge piles all around them. A few weeks later, the wife was invited to be a contestant on a game show. She loves game shows. She won $25,000 dollars during her one-hour appearance on that show. She allowed the money to come from wherever it was at the time and didn't have expectations of where it might, or should, come from. She was open to altering her belief about how the universe works—and that made all the difference.

Some may believe these examples are just coincidences. And that's okay. Others will recognize that quantum physics supports this process, as we'll see later, and they will be able to create what they want more easily.

It may take a while before you retrain yourself to believe money could be created in different ways or that abundance could come to you from anywhere and in any form. We've been taught that money comes from physical printing machines and we must do something to earn that money, and furthermore, according to the mechanistic laws of classical physics, this is how it *appears* the world works, so we believe it. But our beliefs have created that reality. Learning to use the principles in quantum physics instead so we can create differently may take some getting used to, but it's a valuable endeavor and the outcome will be worth the effort.

Until we really understand and accept the new physics, we at least can start moving in that new direction. We can begin taking small steps. We might begin by believing that, even if money is printed on machines, it can show up in ways that don't require hard work. And also that it could come from anywhere.

You'll need to believe that this is possible, however. You can't fool yourself and pretend you believe it could happen when you really don't believe that. If you envision one thing but subconsciously believe something else, that conflicting energy will act like a riptide. The positive energy will flow in the direction of your desire, but your doubtful energy will act like an undercurrent and pull you back the other way. The conflicting thoughts create a tug of war. Your desire and your beliefs must be aligned.

You won't always get what you want, but you'll always get what you believe.

Also, if you subconsciously believe that you don't deserve money, or that you are incapable of having much, or that money is the root of all evil and causes trouble, then you will probably block full prosperity from coming to you. This process applies to everything else you desire as well—not just to money. Your beliefs must align with your desires.

DO YOU WANT TO CREATE SOMETHING ELSE? For instance, do you want to travel? Do you want a new job, a healthier body, or a loving relationship? This process applies to anything and everything. There are no limits to what you can create. There are no degrees of ease or difficulty to what you can create. The only limitations we have are those we believe in. If you believe it's easy to create a job, but challenging to find love, you will experience that outcome.

It's just as easy to create a million dollars as one hundred dollars; both amounts of money are created using exactly the same principle. The only difference in what we manifest is our belief about what is easy and possible, and what is difficult or impossible.

Years ago, I had a strong desire to travel. At that time, I didn't have the funds to travel, so I spent a lot of time working hard, trying to make enough money to go somewhere. Eventually I realized it wasn't the money I wanted. My desire was to visit other places. So rather than just focusing on making money, I envisioned myself traveling. I felt the experience in my physical body. I felt the joy of being in other places. I kept imagining this until it felt real and I knew it would happen.

Within two weeks of envisioning myself traveling, I received phone calls from three different friends. They all wanted me to come visit them and each wanted to pay my airfare. I had manifested trips to Hawaii, Florida, and Oregon by understanding that everything is energy and that imagination directs the form that energy takes. For anyone who feels bad that my *poor* friends had to pay for my trips, one of the greatest gifts I can give my friends is envisioning them as abundant and prosperous. Imagining someone as impoverished or unable to afford something does not benefit that person. Energy can take any form and come to me from anywhere. Infinite energy also flows freely from me as I share abundance with my friends, family, and others. This helps all of us feel abundant and prosperous.

ONE DAY, I HAD A PASSING THOUGHT THAT IT WOULD BE INTERESTING TO VISIT BRAZIL. I had never been there and thought it could be fun. I didn't share that idea with anyone. Actually, I didn't give it a second thought. So even though I only imagined it once briefly, I didn't doubt or resist the idea.

Fear and doubt can counteract your visions. If you struggle and keep *trying* to create something, you're reaffirming that it's not already a reality. You're holding the vision that it's not happening, which will result in it not happening or in its arrival being delayed.

Within a week of this one thought of a trip, my cousin called and asked if I wanted to go with her to Brazil. One of her clients had given her two round-trip, business class tickets to Rio. Needless to say, I wasn't going to turn down that incredible manifestation.

This example shows that you don't need to work hard to visualize something happening; you just need not to doubt it could happen. Doubt works against you.

AFTER I SOLD MY HOME IN SANTA BARBARA, I decided to rent for a while to simplify my life. At that time, two different friends shared horror stories about their desperate search for rentals. Santa Barbara is historically not an easy place to find houses to rent. First, I panicked. I bought in to their beliefs that there was little available, and that those rentals that did exist were outrageously expensive. Once I realized that I was focused on fear and scarcity, I calmed down. Rather than envision a problem, I wrote down a clear description of the home I would live in: the exact view, the number of bedrooms, the rent I would pay, and more.

My friends scoffed at me and declared I was never going to find a rental that fit my "unrealistic" descriptions. But within three days, I was led to the perfect place. It wasn't even on the market yet. I had the impulse to visit past neighbors of mine and followed through on that thought. "Coincidentally" they knew about an upcoming rental right next door to them. And it had everything on my list, including the specific view I had envisioned, the street

I had desired, the number of rooms, and the exact rental price I had listed. I moved in a short time later.

Once my friends learned what had happened, they followed my example. Within days of writing down precise details and holding a clear vision, both found their perfect rentals. After months of searching in fear and desperation, they got what they wanted just days after shifting their focus.

Coincidence? Maybe. Or maybe it's evidence that our thoughts, feelings, and imagination do create our reality. I've experienced too many of these same types of situations to chalk it up to mere chance.

You don't have to believe you have the power to create what you want in your life. Your thoughts and beliefs will still create your reality. Many people believe that God or a loving force is directing their lives, so they just relax and go with the flow. They accept whatever shows up. That works, too. Some believe life is unpredictable and they have little or no control over what happens to them. That belief is fine, if that's what people prefer and it's working for them. Their experiences will still reflect their beliefs about how life works.

Do whatever feels right and works for you. You're an awesome being. The point is that your beliefs create your experiences. The goal here is to help you *easily* create happiness and fulfillment in your life. We're exploring many different ways you can do that. You have amazing powers that can set you free if you choose to use them.

HEALING

One powerful example that shows we have a limited perception of who we are and how life works is the story of Anita Moorjani, author of *Dying to Be Me*. In her book, she describes how cancer ravished her body so completely that her organs finally shut down and she went into a coma. During a near-death experience, Anita learned it was her fear and lack of self-love that had created her cancer. She was shown who she really was and what her life was really about. She was given the choice to return to her body or to continue on to another realm. She chose to return to this realm.[2]

Anita woke up from her coma and a few days later there was no trace of cancer in her body! She was completely healed. Doctors are at a loss to explain this phenomenon. Her near-death experience and her remarkable recovery don't fit into traditional medical doctrine. Anita's experience does, however, offer more evidence that we don't have a full grasp on the nature of reality and that beliefs have more power to create our reality than we've previously understood. Anita discovered the impact her thoughts and emotions had on her body.

Discovering from quantum physics that everything is energy and that my thoughts and beliefs play an inexplicable role in creating my personal reality, I have used that knowledge to heal my body, too. In much less serious circumstances than Anita's, whenever I've experienced a stomachache or any other pain, I focus my attention on that area of my body and remember that it's all just energy. I envision my body relaxing and being perfect, and within moments the pain is gone.

There's one more thing I do. I also ask my body why it wanted my attention, so I can discover if there's any emotional cause behind that pain. The body is the physical expression of our thoughts and beliefs. The body is our barometer. It will reveal what is going on inside of us. I've learned that if I don't deal with the core mental or emotional reason for any *disease* or discomfort I'm feeling then another physical issue will arise to get my attention.

Many in the medical community know about the power of the mind. They have experimented with the placebo effect and the opposite, the nocebo effect. They have seen how people's thoughts and beliefs impact their physical condition, positively reducing pain and illness *(placebo)* or negatively creating illnesses *(nocebo)*.[3]

Since everything is made of energy, we can use our imaginations to heal and shape our bodies. Energy takes the form that we imagine. Cultural beliefs about what affects our health and our bodies have changed throughout history. Currently, we believe that we must eat certain foods and exercise to maintain a healthy body, but that's still a belief. There are many people who have lived to an old age even though they drank and smoked. Centenarian George Burns is an example. And there are many examples of people focused on eating healthy and exercising who have died at a young age from a heart attack. The key was their *beliefs and deeper, subconscious emotional issues.*

Anita Moorjani is a perfect example of someone who was so afraid of getting cancer that she developed cancer. Then her consciousness shifted and her body was completely healed.

Some people claim that illnesses and longevity are results of genetics and heredity. However, some experts question the belief that DNA is responsible for health and physical appearance. They are studying the effects that our thoughts and beliefs have on our bodies, including our DNA. Bruce Lipton, Ph.D., discusses this in his book *The Biology of Belief*.[4] Lipton claims that our thoughts, beliefs, and emotions affect our genes, and that genes can be turned on and off by environmental signals, including thoughts, feelings, and emotions from outside our cells. Dr. Lipton's work focuses on the mechanisms through which energy in the form of our beliefs affects our biology, including our genetic code.

While the debate about which one affects what continues, during the three decades of psychically reading clients I've seen evidence that our thoughts affect our health and that our DNA is just a map that we have created for our bodies. We can change that map. We have power over every aspect of our health and the form our bodies take. This comment is meant to empower you. Again, you are an amazing being with powerful abilities.

Tibetan monks understand the power that consciousness has on the body. They can use meditation to quiet their minds and significantly slow down their bodily functions. Studies have verified their ability to do this. For example, the *Harvard University Gazette* reported in April 2002 that researchers made measurements on practitioners of advanced meditation in Sikkim, India. The article states, "They were astonished to find that monks could lower their metabolic rate by 64 percent. To put that decrease into perspective, metabolism, as measured by oxygen consumption, drops only 10–15 percent in sleep and about 17 percent during simple meditation."[5]

If these monks can affect their bodies by using the power of their minds, then all humans have the potential to develop the same ability. The monks are trained to believe it is possible and that their consciousness does affect their bodies. We, on the other hand, are usually trained to believe we are fragile, subject to diseases beyond our control, and need medical intervention to be cured. We would greatly benefit by accepting our true power to affect our *physical* bodies.

SOME PEOPLE MAY FIND THIS NEXT CONCEPT CHALLENGING and difficult to accept, some may not want to accept it at all, but it may be worth our consideration since we have been limiting ourselves with our old beliefs about reality. So much more is possible.

Classical physicists claim that the universe is mechanistic, that we are mere biological machines that must eventually atrophy, decay, and die. But if we are made of energy, if matter and energy are interchangeable as the quantum physicists claim, then we shouldn't be aging, getting sick, or dying. How could energy age or die? Energy cannot be destroyed; it just continuously changes form. Old age is one of the forms energy can take, but it's not the only form available to us—and energy isn't *required* to take that form. This is a powerful concept, one we should further explore. It could radically change our understanding of health, aging, and death.[6]

If the idea of never dying concerns you, you still have free will. You can leave your body if you choose. Or you could just consciously *transform* your body to light or some other energy form. It does sound like science fiction, but remember that a lot of former science fiction is now science fact. Once we understand how it all works and that everything is energy then we can see we have infinite choices and can create anything. Think of the possibilities we would have if we could grasp that.

Imagine what we could create if we continued to grow wiser while retaining our full life energy. We could create amazing, new, life-enhancing projects for the world.

For people who fear that the planet would become overcrowded and there wouldn't be enough resources to sustain everyone if we all lived as long as we wanted, we can solve this by using our amazing imagination. Necessity is the mother of invention. We are resourceful beings. We can create options to deal with any situation. We could travel to other planets or create alternative resources. We don't need to accept the concept of scarcity. Imagine what we could create if we realized that our resources are also made of infinite energy?

If you fear life would become less valuable or less interesting if we knew we could live longer—or even live forever—think of the fascinating possibilities if you didn't have to squeeze everything into a short eighty-year lifespan.

You could spend more time fully appreciating the different wonders of the world. You could patiently watch a butterfly emerge from a cocoon or watch a spider spin a web for hours without feeling you were wasting valuable time. You could listen to exquisite music for hours at a time without thinking you should be doing something more productive. You could live in a variety of other cultures, create a myriad of interesting projects, and experiment with cultivating many talents—including those you don't have time to develop in one short lifetime.

Maybe you want to be an artist, a chef, a pilot, or something else, but in this brief life you've been limited to one moneymaking career. Rather than spend your precious time feeling exhausted by all of life's demands, you could have a joyful, fulfilling, and adventurous life instead.

There is so much value in changing our perceptions of life and what is possible.

INFLUENCING THE WEATHER

You can extend the power of your thoughts far beyond merely affecting your body. You can influence the weather and your environment. You can experiment, if you like, using these same techniques.

When I arrived in Maui, Hawaii, late one night, the weather report said that it would be raining on the entire island for days. That wasn't the news I wanted to hear. I desired a warm, sunny vacation in Hawaii. I had been studying the effects of our thoughts on our environment so I decided to experiment. Before I went to sleep, I envisioned that the next day we would have clear blue sky. I imagined feeling the warmth of the sun on my skin and relaxing on the white sand beach. I didn't struggle with that vision or doubt that it would work. I relaxed and felt it happening. When I awoke the next day, the sun was shining and there wasn't a cloud in the sky. Excited, I dashed out to the small private beach by my condo and spread out my towel on the sand.

Hours later, something interesting occurred. People started forging their way through the bushes that surrounded my private and secluded beach. Eventually, I was sharing my space with about twenty other people. One couple told me that they had driven around the entire island and found the only spot where it wasn't pouring rain: my tiny beach. They were shocked to discover that from this beach all they could see was blue sky. This confirmed to me that our consciousness is powerful and we can affect the weather as well as our environment.

I've envisioned rain and then watched it rain on my house and not the rest of the city. I have also been successful at bringing the sun out at my home while the rest of the city was shrouded in fog. I've seen people in a drought-ridden area focus so strongly and pray so intently for rain that it actually brought flooding to their area.

A few of us have experimented and been successful with dissipating or *sending* hurricanes away from different areas. I encourage you to experiment with this ability when undesirable weather is predicted for your area. You have to *know* it will happen though. You can't just *wish* a massive storm would go away while secretly doubting your ability to change the circumstances. You will also suppress your ability to influence the weather if you believe some other power knows better than you or that you should "keep out of it" so you don't make matters worse. If you do fear somehow causing damage by changing the weather then it is best that you don't mess with it. Your fear alone could cause a problem. (Remember this discussion regarding the merits vs. the potential negative consequences of influencing the weather when we explore the chapter on parallel universes.)

We're playing and experimenting with our potential.

FOR THOSE WHO PREFER A MORE SCIENTIFIC PERSPECTIVE on this topic we can look at neurobiology.

Neurobiologists believe that the brain uses electrical signals to communicate and send information between brain cells. Our brains are made up of billions of cells called *neurons,* which process and transmit information through electrical and chemical signals.[7] Millions of neurons sending signals produce an enormous amount of electrical activity in the brain, which can be detected using medical equipment such as the EEG. The electrical activity of the brain is commonly called a *brainwave pattern* because of its wavelike nature.[8]

Thoughts and feelings create electrical impulses and currents, which flow beyond your brain to be experienced in the rest of your body.[9] You can feel this energy particularly well when you experience strong emotions. If you're angry, you can feel a surge of energy throughout your body, possibly as an intense heat or sudden burst of strength. If you're heartbroken, you may feel these currents cause a contraction or tightness in your chest. If you are sad or depressed, your body may feel heavy. Those are ways you have no doubt felt these electrical currents affect your body.

While our thoughts and feelings can cause electrical currents to surge through our brains and bodies, this same energy also has an effect beyond the body. If the brain and body are sending electrical impulses and waves of information, how can these waves be limited to the body since the body is just energy? If the body is just subatomic particles and a lot of space, which is what quantum physics is telling us, where are the actual physical boundaries of our bodies?

I've observed the effect these thought waves or electrical impulses have on the aura, the energy field that radiates out from the body. This radiating energy or aura contracts when you are fearful or turns red when you are angry. It also expands when you are excited, happy, or feeling powerful.

These same waves of energy can also affect our environment. These electrical impulses can travel outside of the body, beyond our aura and into the air, much like radio waves being broadcast from a tower.[10] Many of us have been in a room with someone who is angry and felt the intense energy coming from him or her. If you pay attention, when people have been arguing you can feel the tension between them. The air often feels dense or heavy. Likewise, it's often easier to be around people who are happy; their energy feels light and pleasant or warm and loving. We feel comfortable around them.

I realize some people are more sensitive to these energies than others. You may want to pay attention to your own physical sensations next time you are near someone who is enraged, depressed, or excited. Notice how that person's energy affects you.

If these electrical signals can transcend the body to affect you and the environment, might they also affect the weather and the planet? If large groups of people in a particular area are sending out electrical impulses of fear, anger or grief it's bound to affect the atmosphere. Science is discovering that the energy from solar flares affects the Earth and the weather. Why wouldn't massive amounts of electrical energy coming from large populations of people also affect the environment and the weather?

We could learn to use this energy to transmit calm, loving energy through the atmosphere to affect the weather and the Earth in a positive way. Many people subscribe to this ideology, and we've seen positive effects arise from groups of people meditating, chanting, or intentionally sending loving, calm energy into the atmosphere.

One study looked at how transmitting calm energy can affect a region. In July 1993, in Washington, D.C., 4,000 people from sixty-two countries gathered to practice Transcendental Meditation to see if they could effectively lower the crime rate in that area.[11] A final report by a twenty-seven-member independent team of scientists and community leaders found a significant 21 percent reduction in the most violent crime categories during the period of time the group was meditating in the area.[12] Scientists even took into account changes in policing, weather patterns, and all major factors known to affect crime rates when they made their report. They still concluded there was a notable impact on the area. This is an example of the power of consciousness.

Many people may reject the concept that human energy can influence crime rates, the weather, or anything else. Many still subscribe to the belief that we are victims of circumstances, that there are things that are *out of our control.* I trust science will one day verify the effects our thoughts and emotions have on our environment so we can consciously take charge of our experiences rather than rail against nature. We are part of nature. Everything is interconnected.

Maybe some of these examples will help you become even more aware that your thoughts and beliefs are creating your experiences, and help remind you of the importance of being conscious when choosing your thoughts.

How to Create from Energy

Understanding the nature of *physical* reality, that at the foundation everything is energy and our thoughts influence this energy, may make it easier to understand how we can use energy to create what we desire.

If you accept that your thoughts play an important role in your life, but your current circumstances seem too *real,* too convincing, or too difficult to overcome, and if you feel it's too challenging to shift your thoughts and change what you're imagining so you can change your life, then here is a simple exercise to get you started.

Each morning when you wake up, imagine happy little particles of light everywhere around you. See these particles of light joyfully dancing and filling up your room. You can place any feeling you want into this field of dancing particles. What energy would you like to experience in your day: joy and ease, love, success, inner peace, or all of these? Whatever feelings you place in the field will show up for you. Remember to imagine placing these feelings into the field periodically throughout your day. See happy dancing particles of light everywhere. Then notice if your life begins to turn around. It can make you feel happier and safer with life. This is a very simple exercise, but one that can ultimately have a positive affect on your life.

Once you feel more optimistic and capable of consciously creating, then you're ready to go on to the next step. Realize that particles of energy are blinking in and out of existence all around you, all the time. Here is a practical example to help explain this concept: When you're watching a movie at the theater you're actually watching little lights blinking off and on. The lights make it appear as if there are real people moving around on the screen, but that's not the case. You can even get so caught up in the story that you have an emotional response to what you're seeing. But still the images are all just tiny pixels of light. There's nothing solid to those people and events you see on the screen. Similarly, everything in your world is also made of these particles of blinking light. These lights make it appear that everything is real and solid, but it's all just particles of blinking light.

Our minds are very powerful and can create very convincing images. Consider what happens when you're dreaming. When you're having a dream, everything in it feels real—until you wake up. When you're dreaming, your mind creates all the objects, people, and actions taking place. When you wake up you realize that the dream was not the real world after all, it was just an imaginary experience.

At present you believe that this awake realm we're sharing is the real world. However, people who have had near-death experiences report that when they were on the other side, it was this world that seemed like a dream. They say the other side is the real world, and that it is more real than this plane of existence. They explain that this world is an illusion created by our minds. But unlike dreams, where it appears we have no conscious control over what happens, in this realm we can consciously choose our thoughts and therefore intentionally create our experiences.

We've been trained to believe the real world is "out there, separate from us" and we have little or no effect on what happens. But as you'll see, quantum physics says we are interconnected with every object and occurrence in our lives. Our thoughts create our reality. Some physicists are even theorizing that our world may actually be a hologram.[13] This just shows physicists are questioning the nature of reality.

EXERCISES

These are simple steps to create from energy. We actually create everything in our world from energy all the time. We're just not consciously aware that we are doing so. We're now learning how to create consciously and intentionally. This process was created to help you shift your state of mind and practice a new way of thinking.

You may be the type of person who takes action as soon as you intellectually understand concepts. You may prefer visual exercises instead. Or you may do better with exercises that help you to emotionally or physically *feel* the experience. This visualization process is designed to use all the senses to help you learn how to create from energy. You can create a different image and exercise on your own whenever you choose. Do whatever feels easy and natural to you.

When you do this process, take your time. Don't rush anything. Really see and feel the images that emerge for you. Luxuriate in the essence and feeling of what occurs. Taking the time now to use your powerful imagination and deeply feeling your emotions could replace years of hard work.

Step 1. Relax so you can allow this creative process to be easy. Find a comfortable position. Breathe. Slowly take a deep breath and then let everything go. Relax into an even more peaceful state. You are safe. This is easy. Just focus on the sensations of your breath moving in and out.

Step 2. Use your imagination.
Imagine that there are particles of light blinking in and out of existence in the air all around you. Just watch and enjoy them for a while. This really is what is happening. Everything is energy, particles blinking in and out of existence. They enjoy blinking into form. They will take the form that you imagine. They love co-creating with you.

Imagine all the particles emerging from an unseen dimension into the seen world. See your room full of energy, particles of light dancing and playing everywhere in the air. Notice how you feel about these happy particles surrounding you. This is fun and easy. They've always been around you. Everything in your life, everything that exists is created from these blinking particles. The entire universe is made of these.

Now imagine some of these particles joining together and taking the form of $20-dollar bills or the currency of another country. See these bills floating in the air all around you. Imagine other particles coming together and becoming even larger denominations of money, such as $100-dollar bills! See lots and lots of money taking form right in front of you. As the energy emerges from the unseen, it playfully turns into a lot of money. There is money everywhere. Imagine this money floating into your hands. Feel it. Feel the texture. See more of this money lying on the ground all around you. It's all yours. You created money out of the energy that was dancing around you. Energy loves being part of the creative process.

This is one way to create from energy. You imagine all these particles turning into something. They take direction from the pictures you imagine. As you go through your day now, watch for this money to show itself in your personal world. Pay attention, as it could show up anywhere. For example, you could unexpectedly find money on the ground, in your mailbox, or in your bank account. When it does, happily appreciate it and accept it. Smile when it comes to you, knowing that you co-created this money and now you finally have it.

Imagine something else you would like in your life, something you've wanted for a long time. Imagine what it looks like. Then imagine that it's taking form right in front of you. It emerges from the invisible field of energy. If you've wanted love, the image of a person may appear in front of you, or you may feel waves of loving energy emerge and surround you. Feel this love embrace you and fill you with warm feelings.

If there's something else you've wanted—an object, a place, or an experience—all the little particles come together to form that, no matter what it is. It's all easy. See the form become more and more solid. Imagine it becoming fully solid right in front of you. This is yours. Embrace it.

This is a very important part of the process. Imagine having it, touching it, holding it, or surrounding yourself with what you've created. Notice how you feel emotionally. You finally have what you've desired for so long. It's here in your life now. The scene surrounds you. Allow yourself to feel happy or excited or whatever feeling comes up for you. Pay attention to your feelings because they are just as important as your imagination. Your feelings and emotions power the energy that brings what you envision into form.

Enjoy the emotional feeling of having it now. Breathe it in and relish it. Really imagine how you feel having it in your life. Allow yourself the time to fully enjoy it. The reason you've wanted this in your life is for the feeling you imagined it would bring you. So relax and revel in the feelings. Allow your imagination to flow.

Step 3. When you're ready, return to a fully alert state.
Take a deep breath and feel your body—your strong, healthy body. Gently move your body around. What a fun way to create. It seems so easy. This is how nature creates. It goes to the same place to create anything. It draws from the field of energy, and particles that weren't there before emerge into form.

Experts tell us the cells in all living matter grow, divide, and become more—but where does the new matter come from? Where was the matter that is now forming these new cells? How does something *grow* and create new matter? We just take it for granted that something grows, but we haven't questioned what that means or where that new matter comes from. It emerges from the unseen into the seen. And what made it do that? Consciousness. Intelligence.

We've believed for so long that creating something takes action, hard work, and struggle that we now think that's the only way life works. You now have the option of creating by using your imagination and your feelings so that it's simple and more fun. The more you practice this method, the easier and more real it will become.

Once you've fully imagined something, follow through on bringing forth the outcome by trusting your intuition. If it tells you to take some sort of action, this may be part of the manifesting process for this particular item. Your intuition will guide you to where you need to be and what you need to do to have what you just envisioned. The money you just imagined might be in your mailbox or the person you imagined may be at the neighborhood market right now. It's best not to second-guess yourself or try too hard. Just flow with life and trust your inner guidance. And know that whatever you just imagined and created does exist now.

The Science

You may be interested in the physics behind the abilities I've been describing to you, or you may feel too overwhelmed by the incredibly complicated world of quantum physics and not want to learn it. Don't worry, even quantum physicists don't quite know what to make of their discoveries.

"If quantum mechanics hasn't profoundly shocked you, you haven't understood it yet."[14]
—Niels Bohr (1885–1962), Noble Prize-winning physicist

Most of us don't understand the science behind electricity, smartphones, or the Internet and yet we use them. So even if you don't quite comprehend what physicists are saying, you can still develop your abilities. For science enthusiasts, I will list a number of quantum physics sources in the Resources section at the back of the book so you can study these topics in greater detail.

The following concepts can be challenging to grasp, so if you find yourself scratching your head you're not alone. Quantum physics is definitely turning our concept of *reality* on its head. What quantum physics is proving is not only stranger than we think, it also seems to be stranger than we know how to think—at least for now.

First, in order to manifest anything you desire and to understand how you use energy to create, it can be helpful to understand two profound concepts. These are that:

- Everything is energy.
- Our thoughts affect and create reality.

Currently, we're not consciously taking advantage of this information, but it can explain why all these abilities are possible. We'll delve deeper into both concepts so you may learn how you can consciously and intentionally create your world and your experiences.

EVERYTHING IS ENERGY

"The atoms or the elementary particles are not real;
they form a world of potentialities and possibilities rather than
one of things or facts." [15]

—WERNER HEISENBERG (1901–1976), NOBLE PRIZE-WINNING
PHYSICIST

Everything is energy. This is one of the most amazing discoveries in quantum physics. And if we really comprehended the implications of this one concept, our lives would radically change—forever. Since this is not a book on physics, we won't discuss all the details of the physics of matter. Rather than delve too deeply into such discoveries as dark energy and dark matter, we'll just look at the fundamentals. [16]

When physicists probe deeply into matter, they're finding *there is nothing solid to matter*. It is made up of smaller and smaller subatomic particles and a *tremendous* amount of empty space.

People used to think the atom was the smallest building block in the universe. Old illustrations of an atom would look like a small solar system with electrons circling the nucleus like planets circling a sun. But then scientists discovered that the atom was made up of even smaller subatomic particles, such as quarks, leptons, bosons, neutrinos, and more. Everything else was just space. However, they're not sure that these are the smallest units in the universe either so scientists continue to probe and speculate.[17]

They theorized that the Higgs boson or God particle would explain why particles appear to have mass. Now that they've found the Higgs boson, however, they once again realize it still may not explain what gives rise to matter. [18]

There is string theory, the theory that all elementary particles are manifestations of the vibrations of one-dimensional strings.[19] Despite all these theories, however, they still are at a loss to understand how the universe is formed and why there *appears* to be matter since they can't find anything solid to matter.

I had the privilege of spending hours in a one-on-one conversation with world-renowned quantum physicist David Deutsch while I was visiting a friend in England.[20] Deutsch commented that if the building blocks of matter are, in fact, not solid, we must not be solid either—since we are made of them. That makes sense. At what point would *nothing solid* turn solid? If you built a wall with bricks that had no substance to them, then the wall would have no substance either. We might feel the energy charge being emitted from these virtual particles, but we're still just feeling energy, not anything solid.[21]

"Everything we call real is made of things that cannot be regarded as real."[22]
—NIELS BOHR

They've also discovered that empty space is not actually empty. It's teaming with energy! Even a *vacuum* is packed with energy.

This is the definition of matter from Science.NASA.gov: *"The quantum theory of matter says 'empty space' is actually full of temporary ('virtual') particles that continually form and then disappear."*[23]

So there is nothing actually solid or real about matter! What do we do with this information, and how can it change our lives? And why can we apparently see, touch, smell, and taste matter?

FIVE PHYSICAL SENSES

If everything is energy and there is nothing solid to matter, why do we perceive anything as solid—with color, texture, and so on? It may be because we have *trained* our five physical senses to perceive the world that way. Neuroscientists believe that the waves of energy or light that reach our eyes, ears, and other physical senses from the outer world are translated as solid objects and events inside the brain and that's what gives us our perception of reality.[24]

It seems we can't trust our five physical senses to give us an accurate version of the world or of reality, though. Our physical senses deceive us all the time. Science tells us the Earth travels around the sun. Don't your eyes tell you the sun comes up and goes around us? Experts tell us the Earth is round. But when you look around, don't you perceive the Earth as flat, with hills, mountains, and valleys maybe, but certainly not round? The Earth is spinning at approximately 1,040 M.P.H.[25] Do your physical senses feel that speed? Your ears only pick up a small range of sounds. Most frequencies are either too high or too low for human ears to detect. What else exists that you're not hearing, seeing, or feeling?

We would greatly benefit from developing our other senses, including our sixth sense. We also need to open our minds and retrain our five physical senses to perceive the world differently so we can gain a more expanded and, I believe, truthful picture of reality. We have a very limited version of *reality* right now. That's what we're doing now: learning how to shift our beliefs and therefore our perceptions of the universe.

CONSCIOUSNESS CREATES REALITY

Physicists can't figure out why objects at the quantum level, the smallest level, behave differently than those at the large, macroscopic "physical" level since the quantum world is the foundation of the physical world.

On the large or physical scale, objects appear to follow the classical physics principles of cause and effect, laws of motion, and more. But at the quantum level, particles don't follow those same rules. They behave radically different. Particles pop in and out of existence, and they can affect each other at a distance instantaneously without traveling through space and time (quantum entanglement), which brings cause and effect into question. And waves of energy can change into particles when an observer interacts with them.

Physicists are trying to discover a theory of everything that would enable them to connect these two paradoxically different worlds. Some believe that the missing link in their explanations is consciousness. It is consciousness that makes it appear to our eyes that there are solid objects. It is consciousness that creates what we perceive as *reality*.

QUANTUM PHYSICISTS CLAIM that there is no way to prove an objective reality because the observer always influences the outcome of any experiment. Twentieth-century physicists Werner Heisenberg and Erwin Schrödinger both saw a connection between consciousness and reality.

Erwin Schrödinger is well known for his illustration of the principle of superposition, where particles are everywhere and in multiple positions simultaneously.[26] This principle claims that when we do not know the state of any particle or object, then it is actually in all possible states simultaneously, until we check on it. It is the measurement or observation itself that causes the object to be limited to a single possibility.

In a famous thought experiment, which is now known as Schrödinger's cat, Schrödinger imagined putting a cat in a box along with a radioactive substance that, if it decayed, could kill the cat. (Don't worry: No cat was ever actually used or harmed in this experiment.) He explained that it cannot be known if the cat inside the closed box is alive or dead unless an observer looks at the cat. Because of this, Schrödinger concluded that unless someone does look at the cat, the cat must be considered simultaneously both dead and alive.[27]

This contradiction, which defies common sense, is called *quantum indeterminacy* or the *observer's paradox:* The observation or measurement itself affects an outcome. So an outcome, as such, does not exist unless the measurement is made—in this case, unless someone looks at the cat. So consciousness, the observer, is connected with the outcome.

This leads some physicists to conclude that nothing can exist without an observer (consciousness). Albert Einstein didn't like this theory.[28] He believed that the moon existed whether or not someone looked at it. And his view is how we've all been trained to perceive reality. We've been taught that things exist independently from us, that other objects exist whether or not we exist.

But as a result of quantum indeterminacy, there is no way to prove the moon or anything else exists unless someone actually observes it. Nothing can be proven to exist without consciousness.

This is a powerful statement. Basically nothing exists or can be proven to exist without us!

Schrödinger claims that consciousness is an inexplicable part of reality.

"Consciousness cannot be accounted for in physical terms. For consciousness is absolutely fundamental. It cannot be accounted for in terms of anything else." [29]

—ERWIN SCHRÖDINGER (1881–1961),
NOBLE PRIZE-WINNING PHYSICIST

Through his uncertainty principle, Werner Heisenberg posited that one cannot know both the position and the momentum of any particle at the same time. He proved that observing or measuring that particle to learn about either affects the position and/or the momentum of it.

"The 'path' (of the electron) comes into existence only when we observe it." [30]

—WERNER HEISENBERG

So again, the observer affects reality.

Heisenberg is considered to have been an advocate of philosophical idealism. The idealist view holds that nothing has an independent, real essence outside of consciousness, that the objects we perceive are identical with the ideas we have about them, and that it is intelligent life that defines reality. [31]

"Subject and object are only one. The barrier between them cannot be said to have broken down as a result of recent experience in the physical sciences, for this barrier does not exist." [32]

—ERWIN SCHRÖDINGER

This statement suggests something incredible about the nature of reality. We are not separate from anything that we see or experience in life, and there are no boundaries between anything and us. The observer and the observed are one.

If everything is just waves of energy and this energy seems to be aware and becomes particles when someone is looking at it, then what causes the particles to take a particular form? Why do they come together to form a tree or a table or a person? The observer seems to direct or influence the form they take. Grasp the implications and you can create anything![33]

The bottom line is that we're being informed that *everything is energy and consciousness affects or creates reality; furthermore, nothing can be proven to exist without consciousness.*

What do we do with that information and how does it affect our lives?

THE ENERGY THAT IS ALL AROUND YOU AND MAKES UP EVERYTHING in the universe appears to be aware because it reacts when someone looks at it. Thus, to create anything or any experience, you must realize first that energy makes up everything, including the air around you, your body, and everything else you see and experience in the world. Then, understand that your consciousness affects this energy and causes it to take form. Your thoughts, imagination and feelings are the key elements in affecting matter or in creating anything.

It's simple. You just need to imagine this energy taking the form that you desire and then use your emotions to propel your desire into manifest form. Our old beliefs about reality and the mechanics of how life works (that everything is separate from us and we have little or no effect upon those things separate from us) have kept us from knowing we can create in this way.

When Harvard-trained neuroanatomist Jill Bolte Taylor, Ph.D., who professionally studies the brain, had a stroke and the left side of her brain ceased functioning, she experienced a completely different reality. In her 2008 TED Talk, "My Stroke of Insight," she reports that with just her right brain functioning she couldn't distinguish between the atoms of her body and the atoms in space. Taylor was amazed that we, as a bundle of atoms and energy, could move through space and do anything at all. She didn't feel any boundary to her body.

Taylor realized that the brain actually filters out a grander perception of life. She was able to perceive energy everywhere and felt completely expansive; she sensed she was one with everything. She describes feeling she was in nirvana and knew that we as beings exist far beyond our bodies. "We are the life force of the universe," she declares.[34]

There will always be those who believe the world is materialistic and mechanistic and that this was just her brain hallucinating. There are many factors that point to the possibility that she was having an authentic experience, however, not just hallucinating. The concept of non-local mind, for example, supports this type of experience.

In quantum physics, the theory of non-local mind reveals that consciousness is not trapped inside the brain. We will explore more on this subject when we discuss telepathy, psychic abilities, and talking to people who have crossed over. The latter are individuals who have no physical brains anymore, but still exhibit consciousness and have the ability to communicate.

Again, realizing that everything is energy and nothing is solid causes some physicists to believe everything may actually be a hallucination—everything may be a projection or creation of the mind, not synonymous with the brain, as we'll see. If that is true, we can create any experience we want by using the power of our minds and imagining it into existence.

SPIRITUALITY

These concepts show up in spiritual teachings, too. Many spiritual groups practice using the power of thought, prayer, and intention to manifest what they desire. For example, indigenous people around the world perform rain dances and healing ceremonies. Obviously, they know something about the power of thought to affect the weather and their health. It must work or after centuries they would no longer be doing it.

Spiritual masters have been able to multiply fish and loaves of bread from *nothing*, or manifest items like gold, jewelry, or ashes out of thin air. Understanding how everything emerges from pure energy makes these stories believable.

Proverbs 23:7 reads: "For as he thinketh in his heart, so is he." Whoever wrote this biblical passage appears to have understood that your beliefs create your reality.

Traditional teachings report that Christ calmed storms, walked on water, healed the sick, raised the dead, turned water to wine, and more. He said, "the works that I do shall he do also; and greater works than these shall he do" (John 14:12). He also said if we have faith we can move mountains.[35] So are we using our faith, our beliefs to perform such seemingly impossible feats?

Matthew 7:7 reports that Christ said: "Ask, and it shall be given you; seek, and ye shall find; knock and the door shall be opened unto you." This reveals that universal energy responds in equal action to whatever action and energy you put out. It also shows that you don't have to work hard to manifest something. Notice the correlations here:

- *Seeking* certainly takes more time, energy, and action; but if you seek, ye shall find.

- *Knocking* takes less energy; and if you knock, the door shall be opened.

- *Asking* takes the least amount of energy and action; and if you ask, it shall be given.

Many spiritual traditions teach us to allow life to unfold, not to try to control it. It doesn't mean we can't have or create what we want, just that we don't have to force anything or beg for something. Actually, if we feel we have to beg, force, or control, it means we don't believe that the thing we desire is already here now. Believing something is not here now will keep it from being here now. Spiritual masters typically declare something once then leave it alone knowing that the manifestation is already done.

If you believe you are separate from the field of universal energy and you identify exclusively with your ego, the self-described image and definition you have of yourself, you'll probably end up working harder and struggling longer to accomplish your desires. You are not just your ego. You are connected with something much larger: the powerful, loving Source of life. And this intelligent field of infinite energy, often referred to as *All That Is,* moves through you and creates as you, so your ego doesn't have to try to run on its own batteries or try to create by itself.

Just know that you are always connected with this source, align with its powerful creative energy, and then believe that what you desire already exists for you. It's a co-creative action. You're still participating in creating your own reality because you're envisioning what you desire and then effortlessly allowing the universe to bring it into "form." Again, your beliefs about how life works will play out for you: What you believe is what you will experience.

CHAPTER FOUR

INTUITION, TELEPATHY, AND PSYCHIC ABILITIES

"Although attempting to bring about world peace through internal transformation of individuals is difficult, it is the only way."
—DALAI LAMA (1935–), NOBLE PEACE PRIZE WINNER

Here are some more amazing natural abilities that you already possess.

- **You are intuitive and psychic.**
  You can *hear* your own soul and other people's souls, which can help you to understand who you really are and who they really are. You can sense life purposes and what will make everyone happy. You can also sense what beliefs may be preventing you and others from feeling fulfilled.

  Among other things, you can sense who is right for you in a relationship, whether you've met that right person yet, or if a more appropriate person is still ahead for you. This knowledge can prevent a lot of unnecessary suffering. You can know which career will be satisfying, and even where your best job is located. You can sense potential health issues that may not be physically apparent at this time and then prevent them from developing. You can also perceive what fear-based beliefs are causing your current issues and how to heal those.

You can sense what your life will look like if you stay on your current path with your current beliefs, since your beliefs create your reality. And you have free will so you can also change your future if you sense something coming that you don't like, such as an illness, divorce, job loss, or something else. If you want to improve your future, you can sense which beliefs and actions you need to shift in order to create a better outcome.

You have access to information and can receive guidance in all areas of life—past, present, or future—to help you and others live happy, healthy lives. Of course, you can ignore this ability and keep blinders on so you can encounter surprises. But think of the valuable projects you could focus on if unpleasant circumstances weren't draining you or distracting you. Think of the pain and drama you could avoid if you could see different probable futures and head in the best direction.

We no longer need to pretend to be ignorant or that we are helpless victims. There is no value in either. Our souls really do know who we are, our purpose for coming to the planet, and how we can accomplish our original plan. We just haven't been taught that we can reconnect with this information and live fuller lives. We haven't been taught we are powerful creators.

- **You are telepathic.**
You can communicate with people anywhere. Since we are all connected in the *field,* it acts like the *"Worldwide Web"* and enables us to send and receive information through it. You've

probably had the experience of thinking of different people and then, only a short time later, they call you or you run into them. We're actually telepathic beings. We communicate through this field all the time. Most people just haven't been aware that they're doing that.

Amazingly, you can also communicate telepathically with a future love. Everyone is telepathic, so if you'd like to *call in* your future partner, you can talk with that person through the atmosphere, the field. Even if you don't consciously know who that person is yet, your soul knows and can communicate with that person on a deeper level. You can ask that person questions and find out more about him or her. You just need to quietly listen so you can hear the answers. This can also help you feel more comfortable with that person prior to allowing him or her into your life. So many people are afraid of love; they fear being hurt or disappointed, so their fears can actually block love from coming to them. If you have similar fears, communicating through the ethers with your future partner ahead of time can calm your concerns.

Humanity is headed toward becoming fully telepathic. When we know who we truly are and that we are already connected, knowing that we are becoming more telepathic will feel exciting. Once we are fully telepathic, there will be no reason to hide from each other. More trust and compassion will emerge. Fear, guilt, shame, judgment, and suffering will diminish and eventually disappear. That sounds unrealistic right now because we've been taught that humans are flawed and not to be trusted; and we all believe we have secrets to hide. But those insecurities and fears are what caused trouble in the first place.

We're not as far away from realizing our connectedness as many would presume. There is definitely something meaningful emerging in the mass consciousness right now. Even technology is leading us toward telepathy. Social media, smartphones, and the Internet are rapidly increasing our level of connection to one another. Soon even those systems won't be fast enough to please us, so we'll further develop our telepathic skills to connect with each other more quickly.

Our true nature is one of love and connection, not fear, separation, and competition. Survival of the fittest is not how we've survived and evolved. We would have destroyed each other long ago, if that were the case. It's been through cooperation and mutual support that we've survived and evolved.

- **You can see the future of the world.**
  You have access to the *field of consciousness,* a field of energy and information that surrounds and connects us.[1] This field is affecting and also being created by the mass consciousness. The probable future is in that field so you can see what's ahead for the planet. It's better to have the ability to see what's coming so you can do something about it rather than crash into walls and claim ignorance or helplessness. You have free will, so if you see something ahead for the planet that you don't like, you have the ability to affect that future by changing your thinking and your behavior. Your thoughts create reality—so yes, you are that powerful. You are adding to the mass consciousness. We will discuss more about probable realities and the role that beliefs play in creating any particular personal future, as well as the future of the world, in the chapter on parallel universes.

  If you don't believe you have enough power to affect the planet, know that your thoughts and behavior will at least affect *your* reality. If you keep your visions positive, uplifting, and loving, and you listen to your intuition, you may avoid unpleasant occurrences. You may end up being out of town if some disaster hits. If you fearfully imagine disasters, however, you could participate in one of those dramas. Your thoughts, beliefs, and behavior make all the difference. If you believe that unseen forces guide and protect you, then you will experience that. Your experiences are still a result of your beliefs.

If you feel pangs of guilt, like you'd be abandoning people if you were out of town when a disaster hit, you may involve yourself in one of these tragedies to avoid feeling guilty. Wouldn't it ultimately be more beneficial, however, if you were out of town and survived the disaster so you were still alive to help?

It doesn't mean that someone who is involved in a tragedy does so because they have negative thoughts. You may very well allow yourself to be part of a challenging situation so you can help others, or teach them love and compassion.

If enough of us use this intuitive ability, we could possibly prevent many types of disasters and losses of life from occurring. Many of us are already able to sense when something big is coming, such as an earthquake, flood, fire, or hurricane. We can sense a "disturbance in the Force" as Obi Wan Kenobi says in the movie *Star Wars*.[2] We're working on developing our skills even more so we can use them to warn people, or better yet, to change the situation. There is a lot of evidence showing that animals can sense an impending catastrophe. Pet owners around the world report their animals' strange behavior right before a disaster occurs. Look at how elephants and other animals in Indonesia fled to higher ground just before the tsunami hit on December 26, 2004.[3] If animals are able to sense these events approaching, then we have the ability to sense them, too.

There were many people who didn't go to their jobs at the World Trade Center the morning of September 11, 2001. Some intuition must have been at work, even if some people believe it was an angel or another force that protected them. Something inside them still cooperated with that guiding force. Imagine the other benefits that come with being in tune with that sort of guidance.

Developing your intuitive abilities can generate more confidence and trust in life, and it can ultimately help create a healthier and happier world for you and others.

MY EXPERIENCES WITH INTUITION, TELEPATHY, AND PSYCHIC ABILITIES

Some learn best by hearing other people's examples. So I am sharing some of my stories to help you feel comfortable with these psychic and intuitive abilities, to show you that they are real, and to help you see the value in developing these skills. I'm also sharing how I do this process in case it helps you develop your own capabilities. The same steps may work for you. In addition, there will be various exercises to help you shift into these alternate states of consciousness.

People often ask me if I had experienced any signs of my psychic abilities prior to the first eventful night when Rev. Michael Bromley had me read people at his event. After that occasion, I began piecing together episodes of clairvoyance that I had previously dismissed as coincidences. For example, many years earlier there was a week when every night I had troubling dreams of a past boyfriend. I discovered a month later when he called me that he had almost died in intensive care during that same week.

Also, while driving with a coworker after a fundraising event very late one night, her car started acting strangely. We pulled off the nearest freeway exit and shortly after, the engine died. That exit had brought us to a less than desirable neighborhood. Without hesitation, I chose one house in the neighborhood to approach for assistance. The man who answered the door just happened to own an auto repair shop right around the corner. He worked on the car right then and there. Luck? Coincidence? Chance? I realize that these types of *coincidences* happen to me more often than not.

Pay attention to your own experiences. See if similar events have happened to you. You've probably already experienced your own intuitive "coincidences" or psychic episodes in one form or another.

On Christmas Day, 2007, I received a frantic phone call from a client. Her friend's young daughter's plane had gone missing in Panama. I had a houseful of guests so I needed to slip into a back room to quiet my mind. Going from a busy and active state of consciousness to one of a quiet, inwardly focused state took a little while. I was also concerned that I wasn't going to be able to do it. The emotionally stressful life-or-death situation added extra pressure. But this was a very important situation, so I was determined to focus. I wanted to receive accurate and helpful information.

I closed my eyes and became very still. I dropped into a deeper and quieter level inside myself.

You can do the same by becoming very quiet and allowing yourself to drop deeply inside yourself. Closing your eyes and simply being quiet on the surface is different than going deeply inside. By going further inside, you shut out all external stimuli and focus even deeper into the quiet. You can feel the difference. People who meditate often reach that state of deep stillness more easily than those who don't. But it's possible for anyone to become this quiet. When I do this process I connect with a source or consciousness greater than myself, and then ask for help to connect with a particular person.

That day, I mentally asked to connect energetically with the passengers on that small plane. What that means is that I asked to feel as if I was there with them, wherever they were. I didn't feel myself traveling through space to be with them, I just felt myself already where they were—instantaneously. Usually when I do this, I either see myself with them as an observer or I become one of them and see what's happening through their eyes. More often than not, I am the observer witnessing the situation and the environment.

As soon as I calmly asked to be with them, an image appeared inside my mind. It was as if I was watching a movie in my imagination and simultaneously experiencing being a part of that movie. I was on a small plane. I had an image of a pilot and another man sitting in the front seats of the plane. I sensed two young girls sitting in the seats behind the men. This was an example of an ability known as *remote viewing.* I see and experience the situation from my remote location.

The weather was bad, not conducive to flying. We were trying to fly around a mountain, but then I experienced crashing into trees; a lot of foliage was flying past the window. I didn't actually experience the impact, nor did I feel any fear. I was just an observer. The scene suddenly shifted and I knew the plane had crashed. When you access this ability, time doesn't always follow logical rules; just as in dreams, time can jump around and there isn't always a sequential order.

Observing the scene, sadly I knew that the pilot did not survive the impact, and neither did the father and his young daughter. I saw that one of the girls on the plane, however, was still alive. I knew which girl it was. I saw her hair color and felt her personality. I also knew that the search party must find her soon or else she would die from prolonged exposure to the elements.

I spoke with my client and described everything I had seen. She gave me the names of the two girls. I instantly knew which was still alive. My client confirmed my description of her. When they finally found the plane, the only survivor was the girl I had described.

An interesting side note is that the local men in the search party who found the plane reported that they felt guided to the location by a force and a vision that they had. Fortunately, they chose to follow that guidance. The site of the crash was on a big mountain with a lot of trees and foliage, so it was considered a "miracle" that they found the young girl.

We are all capable of much more than we've been taught.

WHILE TUNING IN AND ENERGETICALLY CONNECTING with a young man during a session, I saw an image of his father standing in front of me. To understand what I mean by this, in your mind's eye imagine a plant sitting on a table in front of you. Can you see it in your imagination? You don't actually see something solid in front of you; it's more like an image in a thought realm.

That is how I get images of people when I connect with them. I tend to be a very visual person. I can remember names and other details if I can see them in my mind. You may be more of a sensory person, so you may have a sense or a feeling about someone. Or you may be stronger with your auditory skills and *hear* thoughts or sounds in your head rather than getting a visual image. Learn to trust how the process works best for you.

The young man's father was not actually in the room, but I knew that something was seriously wrong with his health. As I looked at the image of my client's father, I noticed an unusual energy around his body and I *knew* this was not a positive image.

Fortunately, the young man took the information to heart and immediately contacted his father to encourage him to get to a doctor right away. The father heeded the message and went to his doctor. That doctor didn't find anything wrong with him.

But the concerned son insisted his father get a second opinion because his reading with me had been so accurate in other ways. After a long and intensive series of tests, they did indeed discover cancer in the father's colon. The father was told that the cancer was caught just in time, that the tumor would have taken his life if they had not removed it when they did. That occurred in 1990 and the father is still healthy and cancer free today.

We all have free will, so the situation could have turned out differently. I could have doubted myself and not shared what I had sensed with the young son. He, in turn, may have not trusted his intuition or been too embarrassed to tell his father. The father could have chosen to ignore the information since it came from a psychic. On some level, each of us trusted our own inner voices, which resulted in a positive outcome.

THE PROCESS OF ENERGETICALLY CONNECTING WITH ANOTHER PERSON can be challenging to explain. I go into detail with these experiences so you can envision and feel what happens during the process. The biggest reason people struggle with this natural ability is they don't believe they can do it or they don't believe they know how. It may be a new sensation and not one that you've practiced up to now. But if you believe you can learn something new (since you've probably learned many new things in your life already), allow for the possibility that you *can* do this, and also spend time practicing, you may be amazed at how natural it will eventually feel.

You've energetically connected with others before. If you've ever been in a room or watched a movie where someone starts to cry, it may have triggered a resonance with you, causing you to tear up as well. Laughter can also trigger a resonance, as can yawning. We are all connected. It's not just the power of suggestion.

Thoughts and emotions are waves of energy, and they have no boundaries or limits to where they can travel, despite what we've been taught to the contrary. We're usually just too busy to notice these feelings or waves of energy that are being transmitted from another person. When you learn to become still, you may notice that you can feel another person's energy and feelings.

Many of you may experience sadness when there is a global disaster and you think it's just your own personal feelings. However, you may also be picking up the waves of grief in the atmosphere from the masses and not know it. We haven't been trained to believe that's possible. There is an emotional resonance between people, however. We'll look at this further when we discuss the Global Consciousness Project.

As an example of feeling another person's emotions, a few years ago a high-level executive was referred to me because his daughter had repeatedly attempted suicide. Traditional therapy, drugs, and treatment centers were not working, so he was at his wit's end.

When the young teen showed up to work with me, I quietly *tuned in* to her. I felt myself connect or merge with her. I could feel the young girl's emotions, as if I were one with her. Waves of sadness came over me. I felt my heart become heavy. Then I felt her anger and confusion. (Anger usually stems from hurt and fear.) As I allowed myself to delve deeper into her feelings, I knew that she was frustrated because she didn't know what to do with her life. Then an image appeared in front of me. This is a common way for me to receive information. Again, it's like watching a movie, but not in actual physical form; it's more like an imaginary movie is taking place in front of me.

Using another example, so you can sense what this means, imagine holding a green apple in your hand right now. Really "see" the shape, size, and color of the apple. When I see an image, it's similar to that way of seeing. It's not in physical form, but I can still see it. It's not inside my head; it's in space right in front of me.

I didn't tell myself what to imagine while I sat with the girl, however. The images in this movie just came to me; they were being transmitted to me from the girl's consciousness. When you practice with this ability, learn to allow images to be transmitted to you. You won't need to force them, they will appear to you. You'll just need to learn to open up and receive them, then trust the images and thoughts you are sensing.

The girl's soul was showing me who she really was, what was bothering her, what would make her happy, and what her best life direction would be. I saw an image of her helping animals. I could emotionally feel her connection and empathy for animals, and knew that she mistrusted most people. As the image continued, a solution to her dilemma was revealed. I saw how she could make this particular life path happen and the steps she could take to bring this vision into form. I was seeing a probable reality that her soul desired and was projecting to me. The vision revealed a version of her life that was available to her if she chose that path.

When I shared with her what I was seeing, the girl's eyes lit up as if she was finally being recognized for who she really was, and she was finally receiving permission to live true to her heart. She now had a dream to pursue. I continued to put words to her feelings in a way she herself had been unable to express to others. The loss of her dream had caused her anger, fear, and depression. She thought it wasn't realistic or possible to achieve. Now she was excited to start researching schools where she could study her true passion.

After our time together, her father called to say there had been a dramatic shift in his daughter. She stopped attempting suicide. Her noticeable change had such an impact on her father that he then came to me to find the path to his own happiness. Shortly afterward, he quit his high paying, prestigious job and began working in a field that had been calling his heart for years. He started working for a charitable non-profit organization.

These are examples of how a *psychic* ability can help others; it can dissolve pain and suffering and even save lives.

IT CAN BE DIFFICULT TO TELL THE EXACT TIMING that something will occur in the future for two main reasons. First, when you have a vision of something that will occur in the future, the vision can often appear to be taking place in the present; it can appear to be happening now. Second, people have free will and they can affect the timing. Their fear can cause something to take longer; or their strong intention and commitment can speed things up and cause it to happen sooner. To know about the timing, I usually ask inside and listen to the answer that arises. Often a specific month or year will pop into my inner vision. Timing is still connected with a person's free will, however; it's influenced by the person's level of fear, or a clear and unwavering commitment to having it happen sooner.

ONE WOMAN WANTED TO KNOW ABOUT HER LOVE LIFE. She really wanted to be married. I saw a very clear image of her future husband, including his brown hair and beard, his personality and mannerisms, and the ranch he was living on in either Montana or Colorado. (These states often have similar appearances, so it was tough to tell where that ranch was.) This time, I even heard his name fly quickly past me, which is not a common detail for me to pick up—although it does happen from time to time. When names do flash before me, they are often very unusual names, so it would be challenging for someone to enact a self-fulfilling prophecy based on the name. I also heard, as a thought that arose in my mind, that this man would have lost his previous wife to cancer.

This client attempted to make every guy she met be that future husband, but it never worked out. She even found guys with his particular name, but it was never the right one. Then finally, she met the exact man I had seen in my vision, with the same name, appearance, mannerisms, and location, *and* he had lost his previous wife to cancer. They were married within a few months.

WHEN I BEGAN THIS WORK, the most challenging part of the experience was being brave enough to say out loud what I was hearing inside. Fear of being wrong, criticized, and humiliated can stop a lot of people from exploring their abilities. But have faith. Do your best. The critics can't harm you. And if they try, don't let them (that includes you, as your own worst critic).

"Great spirits have always encountered violent opposition from mediocre minds. The mediocre mind is incapable of understanding the man who refuses to bow blindly to conventional prejudices and chooses instead to express his opinions courageously and honestly."[4]

—ALBERT EINSTEIN

Many of us have already broken through the fear of being judged and ridiculed. Skeptics no longer affect us or stop us. We have faced potential embarrassment and been successful anyway. And there are many of us out in the world now being psychic and intuitive— bettering our lives and using these abilities to help people. So now the way is open for you. You're free to explore and experience your own true potential. You don't need to be perfect. We've proven these abilities are real, so now you can just relax and experiment with them.

Apparently when you were young, before you learned to doubt yourself, you didn't let any fear of failing or other people's opinions prevent you from learning to walk. You just went for it. Maybe you can use that same adventurous and determined spirit to help you develop and apply these new skills.

I began my psychic journey by being *thrown into the water*. Maybe you will choose to develop your abilities intentionally. We all have different paths that lead us to the emergence of our abilities. Trust your personal path. And while you don't need to develop any of these skills if you have no desire to do so, hopefully you won't deny them because of fear, insecurity, or an attachment to old limiting beliefs. There is so much more awaiting you in life if you will be courageous, explore, and take chances. You are much more powerful than you know. And life can be more magical and more fun if you will believe that.

HOW TO DEVELOP YOUR INTUITIVE, TELEPATHIC AND PSYCHIC ABILITIES

It's helpful to understand consciousness and the role it plays in these abilities. All these skills are possible because of consciousness. Mainstream science doesn't actually have a clear understanding of what consciousness is yet, so most scientists ignore the topic or claim it is simply a result of activity generated in the brain. Consciousness is not limited to the brain, however. It extends well beyond the physical body, as we'll see when we discuss non-local mind. Whether or not science can explain it, we all know we are conscious and have awareness. What consciousness is capable of achieving is the real topic of interest here.

There are different states of consciousness, and each has its own brain wave or energetic frequency.

- Awake

- Daydreaming and deep relaxation

- Light sleep and meditation

- Deep, dreamless sleep and Transcendental Meditation

- Lucid dreaming

- Intuition and psychic ability

- Spiritual channeling and consciousness beyond this realm, not limited to the body

- And maybe more that we haven't discovered yet

What are the steps you take to shift from one of these states of awareness to another?

Actually, you already know how to shift into different states of consciousness. You do it all the time. So let's see if you can allow the process of shifting into an intuitive or psychic state (or any other on the list) to be easy, too.

You frequently shift from an awake and alert state of awareness, focused on what is happening at that moment, to daydreaming. Your mind starts drifting and imagining being somewhere else, such as on a beach in Hawaii or back at work talking with a coworker. Sometimes you consciously imagine being somewhere else, but more often than not your mind drifts without you consciously being aware of it.

You know you can intentionally shift from daydreaming to the fully awake state by snapping out of it and purposely focusing your full attention on the present again.

You have practiced being awake and alert, and you have experienced daydreaming many times, so they're both familiar states of consciousness. It's easy to shift from one to another.

You shift from being awake to the sleep state by calming or relaxing your mind. This is another familiar shift in consciousness for you.

You can also intentionally shift from your awake state to a more intuitive or psychic state by quieting your mind, not paying as much attention to the outer world, and not allowing your mind to chatter about other things, including any fears that you "can't do this." You shift your attention and listen instead to a subtler, deeper voice inside you. Once you begin accessing this state of consciousness, you can sense a difference in how it feels when you shift into it. It can be subtle, like falling asleep. When you're falling asleep, you're not quite aware at what point the shift happens between being awake and being asleep; you don't know the actual moment you fall asleep. It's a subtle shift.

Similarly, don't expect a dramatic shift in consciousness when you move into the intuitive or psychic state. It will usually be subtle. You'll know you've reached it when you start sensing feelings or information coming to you. In this altered state of consciousness, you'll be connected to a much more expansive field of information, and knowledge can easily rise to your awareness. The trick is learning to trust the insights that arise from that quiet, altered state. Unfortunately or fortunately, depending on your perspective, the ability to pick up psychic information is similar to the ability to imagine. So at first you may fear you're imagining the information you're receiving.

When you begin shifting into this expanded state of consciousness, notice how you feel. It's usually a strange combination of feeling relaxed and almost like you're daydreaming, but simultaneously you're aware of information coming to you from another realm. You just know something. You are aware of information that is not physically apparent.

At some point, compare that feeling with how you feel when you are imagining something. With practice, you'll be able to sense the difference between the two.

Throughout your life, you've been able to check inside to ask yourself if you wanted to do something. For example, a friend asks you if you want to go to an event with her. You shift your attention inside and sense how that feels. You get an image of the future with that choice and if it feels pleasant, your answer is, "Yes, I'd love to go." This intuitive ability is the same ability we're talking about. You can go to that same place inside to get intuitive feelings and information.

With this psychic ability, however, there is an additional element to it. Your mind may tell you to go because you remember a past experience. You then project that experience on this current one and imagine it will also be fun. However, when you connect with your enhanced psychic ability, something inside you may feel uneasy about this event. You may pick up information on a subtle level that says attending this event won't be a positive experience. There may be trouble brewing at this particular event that your soul knows about and doesn't want to be a part of it. Or possibly you may be needed at home that evening, and although your ego isn't aware of this fact yet, your deeper self senses it.

Picking up all these subtle messages means that you're listening on a more expansive scale now. You're tuning in to the field of consciousness to pick up information that is not physically or logically apparent. Your deeper consciousness, the part of you that is always connected to a higher consciousness, really does know who you are, what will make you happy, and how to achieve that. Take the time to listen and to trust that inner voice. Then act on what you hear.

You have to believe this is possible to do. Then relax, listen, trust, and acknowledge what you sense. Practice this state of consciousness.

You can go to this same deeper and quieter place to gather intuitive or psychic information about other people, too. Practice by asking a friend a question and sensing the answer before the person responds out loud. You may want to begin with simple questions that can be answered yes or no. There are some exercises later in this chapter that may help you reach this state more easily.

ONE OF THE ASPECTS OF USING THIS ABILITY to help yourself and others is learning to trust what you're sensing, and then being brave enough to share that information with someone. Many of us have a fear of being wrong. But the more you share what you see and hear with a supportive person who can give you feedback, and the more you learn to take action on what you hear, the better you become at using this ability. When you correctly *get* an insight, you'll eventually learn how that feels or "clicks" inside you. When you miss something or misread it, you'll eventually know how that feels, too. For instance, it might feel heavy or empty.

You'll also discover you can't trick yourself into believing something that you really don't believe. You'll eventually learn to sense if you're right. It just becomes a matter of subtly adjusting your intuitive dial. But if you don't practice and get feedback, whether it's feedback from another person or from actually seeing the outcome, you won't grow.

You've learned everything you do in life by practicing. You practiced walking, talking, eating, and so on. Remember, intuition is a natural ability. You weren't worried that your eyes would get it wrong when you started seeing, and you weren't afraid that your mouth would say it wrong when you first started talking. You just did it. Your inner senses are actually more trustworthy and accurate than your outer eyes and ears. The only thing that could hold you back is your own doubt and hesitation. Breathe, trust, and play with it. Allow it to be an interesting adventure.

Or you could just wait until everyone else learns to do it and be one of the last ones to develop this ability. That may be a safer way for you to go. You may be more comfortable waiting until everyone else proves this is a real ability. That's okay. We all develop at our own rate. Be easy on yourself. We're all in this together.

If you don't like being told what to do or don't want to be left behind, my previous suggestion may have had an interesting effect on you. It may have inspired you all the more to learn to be intuitive or psychic. Many of us enjoy being the rebels or the explorers. If you are someone who doesn't want to miss out on any fun, when I suggested you be the last one to develop this ability it probably made you want to jump in and be one of the first to try it.

EXERCISES

When you do the following exercises, remember that everyone has different modes of learning. You may be a visual person who can easily see images or pictures in your mind. Or you may be better at hearing information, or receiving thoughts, in your mind. You may be the type of person who experiences emotional feelings about something. Or you may feel physical sensations in your body: tingles, chills, gut feelings, or something else. You may experience a combination of any of these. We'll use a variety of these in the exercises so you can find something that works for you. Trust the style that is best for you.

Here is a method you can use to access your visionary or sensory abilities. Think of a choice you need to make between two different options. Now imagine you are at the apex of two different paths that form a "V" shape, with one path going off to the left and the other to the right. Imagine one option lies on the path to the left and the other option on the path to the right. Close your eyes and imagine walking down the path on the left, keep walking ... and walking ... and walking. Notice what you see, hear, or feel on that path.

Keep walking. Make sure you walk far enough to get a real sense of what happens on that particular path. Once you've walked far enough and you know how you feel and what you've seen or heard then return to the apex of the two paths.

Now, imagine yourself walking down the path to the right and keep walking ... and walking ... and walking. Notice how you feel, what you see, and what you hear on this path. Walk far enough down this path to get a clear sense of the results and consequences of going down this path.

Your greater self knows which direction will make you happier and is ultimately better for you. By doing this exercise, you can see the future outcome of each choice before you actually take physical action.

If you're a visual person, this next exercise will be very simple for you. It's an easy and effective way of seeing your future. First, we'll use the analogy of being in a helicopter above a city looking down at the streets below. From that higher perspective, you have the ability to see where your car is and what traffic or obstacles are ahead for you. You have the ability to see what you will encounter if you continue down that particular street.

In the same way, if want to see your future and you're good at visualizing, you can imagine lifting yourself up above your life, seeing yourself high up in the clouds, and looking down at the future that is ahead if you stay on your current path. If you're happy with what you see, then you can continue on your path. If, however, you see something unpleasant, you can change your direction. I know of one woman who decided against marrying someone by using this method. When she floated above her life and looked down at her future, she saw that she was not happy in the marriage. You intuitively know the truth despite your ego's attempt to pretend everything is fine. This exercise is one way to access your intuitive knowledge.

THIS NEXT EXERCISE IS DESIGNED TO HELP YOU shift into an altered state of consciousness and move out of your analytical mind so that information can come to you from an expanded level of awareness. The images can remove your mind chatter so that you are able to access information at a different level. You can use this guided process for now. Later on, you can personally create whatever images work best for you.

Step 1. Relax and become quiet.
Sit in a comfortable position. Take a deep breath and fully relax. Allow everything to become quiet. . . . Breathe again. . . . Take your time. Allow yourself to feel the process and imagine the visuals. Trust that the Universe supports you. . . . Relax and trust. If it's easier for you to relax and imagine things with your eyes closed, then later, once you learn how to do this exercise, have your eyes closed.

Step 2. Connect with Source.
Imagine a loving ray of beautiful white light coming down from the heavens and entering the top of your head through your crown chakra. Open up and receive this beautiful white light. It brings you knowledge from a higher source. See and feel this white light flow inside you and gently move down through your head like warm, flowing water.

As the light flows to the middle of your forehead, just above your eyebrows, imagine the light opening up your third eye, your inner eye. See a beautiful, full beam of light coming out of your forehead like light from a lighthouse and spreading out further and further into the world. It is a radiant and expansive light. See it become brighter and brighter. See it spread out even wider and going farther, and growing brighter, as it expands. With your third eye wide open and this loving light pouring forth from it in front of you, know that you have full knowledge of anything that this light touches. Breathe and see the beauty and wonder of the world before you.

Keeping your third eye open and the light pouring out, see and feel the rest of the white light continue down through your body. Feel it flowing further inside you, continuing into your throat. The light soothes and heals everything it touches. Now, see the white light open up your throat chakra and send light out from you, like a beam from a lighthouse going out into the world. See it spreading out further and wider. See it become more beautiful and even brighter. You can trust that anything that comes from your voice now will be loving, compassionate and helpful.

Take a deep breath and relax even more deeply.

The white light inside you continues to gently flow further down through your body, loving and healing everything it touches. As it reaches your heart, it opens your heart and chest, and sends a loving ray of light out into the world. See the light like the beam from a lighthouse spread out in all directions, sending more and more love out to the world. You now have full knowledge of anything that comes in contact with this light. You know the true essence of people and other living things; you know their souls' journeys and their reasons for being here. And with this love you feel compassion and support for all things.

The white light inside your body continues to flow like a warm, loving waterfall further down and into your solar plexus, into the middle of your body. As that area slowly opens up, beautiful white light streams out from it. It streams out wide like light from a lighthouse. See it radiating out with love. Now, in return, the universe sends a loving and powerful ray of white light into your solar plexus. Rays of light now come in to you from all directions. These wonderful rays of light bring supportive energy that empower and strengthen you. You feel a strong sense of self-confidence. You are exchanging light and energy with the universe. You can use this powerful energy to co-create wonderful projects in the world. This loving power fills you and sustains you.

As the white light inside continues to fill you, it flows into your lower abdomen, your creative center. White light fills you with incredible creative ideas. Your creative ideas can touch the world. You can access this wonderful light any time you want to create anything.

The light continues down through the lower part of your body, to the base of your torso, and into your legs, knees, ankles, and feet. Feel this magnificent energy flow from the lower part of your body, through your legs, and out through the bottom of your feet into the ground to help you connect with the earth. Now see a powerful beam of light come up from the earth and enter into your feet, legs, the base of your torso, and up into the rest of your body. It gives you strong support to keep you healthy and connected. As you send loving and grateful energy into the earth, it sends beautiful, strong, and supportive healing energy to you. You are blessing and healing each other.

Imagine beautiful white light filling you and radiating out from every part of your body. See this light surround your entire body. See the light becoming whiter and brighter. Take a deep breath in and slowly exhale. See the light radiate out from you and extend further now in all directions. See it filling your room. See the light grow brighter and more radiant. Your entire room is filled with the white light that radiates from you.

Now, take a deep breath and see the light expanding even further, going beyond your room and out beyond the entire building. See the light becoming even brighter and more brilliant.

Imagine this loving white light expanding and expanding, until it encompasses the entire Earth.

See that powerful light continue to expand out to the stars and the planets. It expands to fill the entire universe. See the light connecting everything.

Take a deep powerful breath in . . . and then slowly exhale.

Know that this light is the essence of who you truly are. Everything that this light touches is part of you. You have knowledge and loving awareness of everything and everyone that is touched by this loving and expansive light. You are love and light.

Continue to relax deeper into this beautiful and expansive state of being. This is where answers and visions can show themselves to you.

Step 3. Ask for guidance.
In this quiet and relaxed state, ask your source or guides to show you the highest information for the best, most loving outcome.

Now, quietly ask your questions. What do you want to know? If you want to see anything in your future, this is the state of awareness that can show that to you.

See or sense yourself five years in the future and witness the picture that appears. Just relax and allow a scene to arise before you. Notice everything you can. Where are you? How do you feel? Is anyone else in this scene? Allow the picture to arise easily. You don't need to force it or make it happen. It will just appear. You may get one simple picture or you may see an entire movie flow before you. Either way, you can feel the answer and whether or not it's a positive image.

If you experience an answer that you don't like, ask what you can do to change the situation. What do you need to know or do to shift to a different path that will lead you to a happier outcome? The answers will come to you. Trust. You are loved and supported and can live your best life. You're receiving guidance on how to do that.

You can also hear thoughts in your mind giving you information. Notice what those thoughts are. When you are in this relaxed and open state of mind, you can dialogue with this guiding source. You can ask and receive information. Just be quiet enough for the answers to surface. You'll know or hear them easily.

If you want to know something about a person, imagine that person in front of you. If you can't get a visual picture of that person, it doesn't matter. Just feel that person's energy in front of you. Then feel energy connecting you with that person as if you've joined their essence. Just relax and feel. Notice what emotions you feel or any information that arises in your mind. Ask a question and quietly listen for the answer to come. Ask another question and listen. Or just be still and patiently wait for information to arise.

If you feel yourself starting to analyze or that you're trying too hard, just calm down, breathe, and go back into that relaxed state of being. Take your time. You can also imagine the white light coming down from the heavens and entering into the top of your head again. See it bringing you valuable information. Keep your crown chakra, the top of your head, open so you can stay connected.

This is this same state where you can telepathically talk with others. Keep the same expansive awareness and imagine being in front of any person you want. Then in your mind, talk with him or her. We're all connected. We all exist within an energy field. Remember consciousness is unlimited. It expands way beyond the body; it can travel anywhere and connect with anyone. If you know that this person is in another city, feel your consciousness be in that location and sense yourself with that person. Then tune in to that person: become still and notice what you hear, feel, or see.

You can stay in this state of awareness for as long as you want, asking as many questions or seeing as many visions as you can. Your consciousness can be anywhere, including the future.

When you are ready, you can move to Step 4.

Step 4. Return to a fully awake state.
Slowly take a deep breath in. You are a beautiful being. Notice physical sensations in your body again. Feel the bottom of your feet. Slowly move and stretch your feet. Feel physical life energy move up your legs and into your body. Slowly move your body around. Feel strong life energy move up your body, through your chest, and down into your arms and hands. Gently move your neck and head from side to side. Feel life energy fill your neck and head.

Take a deep cleansing breath. Just sit and relax for a while. Gaze around you and see the glorious beauty that is your world.

This exercise can help you remember you are connected with everything. You can become completely aware of anything you focus on. Any time you want to connect, to know anything—about the past, the present, the future, other people, or anything—this is what you can do to connect with it.

YOU CAN USE THIS SAME PROCESS to access the global consciousness and see where the world is headed. When you want to access that information, be somewhere quiet so you can calm your mind and connect with the energy field that is around you, which contains all information. Believing that this field of information is somewhere far away or difficult to access is what keeps most people from connecting with it. The field is all around you and it pervades you. You are a part of it, so you have easy access to it.

Once you still your mind, you can gently ask inside to be shown something in particular. For example, you can ask to be shown whether or not there will be a lot of precipitation in your area this winter or who will win an election—or any other information you want to know. You can practice connecting with this field and obtaining information, visions, and more any time you want. And you can get validation about this information by watching what actually occurs in the world, depending on how far into the future you went. Timing for events can be tricky. All time is simultaneous time from the perspective of the field, however, so you may see everything happening at once. Also, people have free will, so events can change.

THE BENEFITS OF DEVELOPING YOUR INTUITIVE, TELEPATHIC, AND PSYCHIC ABILITIES

Accessing your intuition and connecting with higher guidance has many benefits and practical applications to improve your life and the lives of others. Along with other benefits, it:

- **Makes life easier.**
  Connecting with and being able to hear your higher self, Source, or whatever word you choose to use for that which you contact for guidance and direction, will always help your life. It can ultimately lead to more trust and happiness. The

happier people are, the more loving they often become and the more positive influence they have on those around them.

Becoming lost and confused, or taking a path that causes frustration, hurt, or anger doesn't usually benefit you or anyone around you. It causes unnecessary suffering. For those who believe suffering is essential for learning, there are also easier ways to learn. Hasn't the world suffered enough? You have free will, though, so if you truly believe that you personally learn better by suffering, trust your intuition. Ultimately, you know what works best for you.

If you're concerned that this expanded awareness could take away spontaneity or surprises in life, know that you always have the option to ignore your inner voice so you are able to be *surprised*. But at least you will have the option. Most people don't know they have a choice. Most blindly feel their way through life, all the while fearing they could make a mistake or that terrible things could be lying in wait for them just around the corner. This intuitive ability helps to create more confidence and inner peace.

Accessing your intuitive abilities can put you in the right place at the right time. Life then becomes easier, more fun, and fascinatingly filled with synchronicity.

- **Reduces fear.**
  You'll be able to trust more and therefore allow the life force to move more freely through you. Fear can prevent us from experiencing joy and love. The fear of failure, criticism, or loss can prevent us from fully living life, as it often causes us to withdraw and live small. Learning to trust, to believe in ourselves, and to journey beyond our fear-based restrictive boundaries can help us more fully enjoy life!

  Concern that no one will ever love us is an example of something that could cause us to make poor choices. We could tolerate unloving or abusive behavior from someone who isn't right for us because we fear being alone. *Knowing* that there is someone better who will love us, and that he or she is already on the way into our lives, can help us relax and enjoy life in the moment.

If you absolutely knew that life was going to work out for you, wouldn't you be less stressed? If you absolutely knew that a certain path would cause you pain and heartache, and that an alternate path would bring you joy, wouldn't you choose to travel that better path?

I acknowledge that there are *adventurous* souls who might intentionally choose the more difficult path for the sake of a challenge, just to see if they can overcome obstacles and become stronger. Believe it or not, we've all chosen the tougher path at some point, even though on an intuitive level we knew it would be the more challenging path. We are curious and adventurous souls and sometimes for some those paths are more exciting.

Trusting your inner voice, that part of you that is in touch with Universal Intelligence can help you make better decisions. It's always your choice, however.

- **Helps others.**
Tapping into expanded awareness is a way that you can help others. We can all help each other. When people around you become lost or confused, you can use this ability to help them reconnect with their best paths.

Do you know the difference between *trauma* and no *big deal?* Trauma is when something upsetting is happening to you. No big deal is when that same upsetting situation is happening to someone else. You may have compassion for others, but you are not as personally traumatized by their situations as you are by your own circumstances. In other words, when you become emotionally charged by your own circumstances, you don't always think clearly. You can't always see the solution. When something is happening to others, however, you can more easily see what they should do to solve their issues, such as change jobs, speak up, leave a dysfunctional relationship, or face their fears. It's easy to give someone advice when you're not the one who has to face the fear of dealing with that situation.

You can use your intuitive ability to help people reconnect with their true selves, to hear their inner voices again—if they ask you for such help—so they can find their way out of confusion. You will usually be confirming what they already know deep inside anyway. Accurate information will resonate with them. You can even tune in to people who are not in your physical presence and still help them.

If you fear you are invading people's privacy, of course you can always ask them for permission first. Understand that ultimately we are all connected; we're here to love and support each other so we already have deep soul knowledge of each other anyway. We're not as private or hidden from one another as we'd sometimes like to believe. No need to fear this connection though. This ability actually generates more compassion for self and others, not more judgment. Remember, fear and mistrust can keep us from living our true potential.

You can talk with a person's personality or ego, but you'll always gain better insight from the soul. A person's ego may resist being accessible, but the person's soul is always open and knowledgeable. The soul will sense the compassion that is authentically generated by this ability. So when you connect, ask to communicate with the person's soul or higher self, not the person's ego or personality. You'll be able to sense the difference. The soul has deeper and wiser information. When a person hears the information that comes from the soul, it will have a deep resonance to it. People may not hear what they're hoping or wanting to hear, but they'll sense on an intuitive level that the information is true.

If you ever share psychic information with people, always emphasize free will. They get to create their lives anyway they'd like—and they may not want to hear information from you. It's always their choice. We want people to be empowered and guided by their own inner sources. And we want the same for you. If they can hear their own inner answers, encourage them to trust those.

Here is a powerful way you can help others by using telepathy. Realize that when you worry about loved ones (because we've been taught that worrying about others proves we care) you're actually *sending* them fearful and unhealthy visions. They may telepathically pick up your worrisome and pessimistic visions, which could add to their problems. Your fearful thoughts and visions could feed their fears. So to truly help people, use your imagination to send them positive thoughts and happy images telepathically. They will receive those visions, which can help them create those experiences instead. The best gift you can give people is to believe in them. Trust that their souls know what they're doing, even if it appears that their personalities or egos don't have a clue.

- **Improves health.**
Trusting your own inner voice can help reduce fear and stress, which ultimately can prevent many diseases. Listening to that same voice can also help you sense if stressful energy is beginning to take physical form in your body. Recognizing and releasing that fearful energy can prevent it from becoming an illness.

Being able psychically to see people's physical conditions, and possibly uncovering the deeper emotional issues behind the conditions as well, can enable them to heal physically and emotionally. In some cases, using this ability can save lives.

THERE ARE MANY OTHER REASONS why developing these abilities can enhance your life and the lives of others. You can probably imagine some I haven't mentioned. My friends and I have used our abilities to help each other find misplaced objects such as keys, wallets, airline tickets, and more. These skills can even help people find missing loved ones. This is a loving and compassionate way to help people.

If you worry that you might become overwhelmed by too much psychic information, or you fear you are too sensitive and could take on the pain of others, it's important to know that you have the ability to shut it off. You can either consciously say, "Enough. I'm done for now," or you can imagine turning off a light switch. You can surround yourself with white light or develop some other protective image that works for you.

You are not at the mercy of your psychic abilities. You have free will, you are sovereign, and you can control them. The fear of becoming overwhelmed comes from victim consciousness. We have believed in the concept of *victim* for too long. It's time to move beyond it to knowing that we are empowered creators.

FREE WILL

People have free will. In the stories I have shared thus far, I sensed certain details based on the future people were creating with their thoughts and beliefs (even if their beliefs were hidden in their subconscious minds). All of these people could have changed their futures—and some did once they received helpful guidance from their souls. I just became the megaphone so the inner voice could be heard. If I could hear what their souls knew, they themselves had access to their souls' wisdom, too.

My intention always is to help people, to give them information that will improve their lives, and to bring them more happiness. I strongly believe in, and therefore emphasize, free will.

I encourage you always to trust your own intuition first. When you receive psychic or intuitive information, it should resonate with you and confirm what you sense deep inside. The majority of people validate that the information they receive from intuitive people, or "sensitives," is what they've already thought or sensed. For example, anytime I've seen someone headed for divorce, that person has already sensed it, too. If we see something we don't like in their future, we can discover the solution from their souls so they can change that future.

People still have free will and they can do what they want. Many times, the people who sensed they were headed for a divorce were able to hear the guidance and act on it. The information enabled them to save their marriages. Other times the people weren't interested in saving their marriages so they continued on the path to divorce and onward toward new life adventures. Free will is a key element in what people do with the information they receive.

I saw that one young woman was headed toward developing breast cancer. I could see that the anger she was carrying toward her father was *eating her up* and there was a high probability that the energy would take physical form inside her. (In the decades that I've been doing this work, my experience has been that 99 percent of health problems have mental and emotional issues underlying them. For people to improve their physical health, it's also important for them to heal the emotional and mental issues that have created their problems.)

I saw an energetic blockage developing in that woman's breast. But I also knew what she could do to release that anger so that it never turned into a physical tumor and I gave her instructions about precise actions to take so she could heal psychologically. Those steps included seeing a therapist.

Unfortunately, four years later the young woman returned, admitting she hadn't taken any of the recommended steps and had developed breast cancer. We started working with her options from that point going forward. There are always solutions, no matter which path you've chosen or what situations develop in your life.

Another woman with intense anger toward her abusive father had been declared cancer free by her doctors after a series of chemotherapy and radiation treatments. However, I sensed that the emotional issue that had caused the cancer in the first place had not been dealt with, and that the cancer could reoccur. This information angered her, but she vowed vehemently that she would never forgive her father. The cancer did return. Sadly, she did not survive it that second time. It's interesting to note that her family had sensed she was struggling with an issue regarding her father and they, too, were concerned that her cancer could return for that reason.

ACCURACY

When you begin exploring your abilities, understand that no intuitive or psychic can be 100 percent accurate with predictions because people have free will. People can change their futures by making different decisions. That's why I always tell people that *if* they stay on their current course with their current beliefs, this is where they are headed.

The fear of being wrong or failing has stopped many people from living their best. Perhaps you'll see that trusting yourself and living fully can lead you into much more interesting life experiences, whether you're right with your intuition all the time, or not. It's certainly done that for me.

It might also be helpful to know that I've had people tell me that when they left our private session they thought I was completely wrong; they were certain that their paths were not going to go in the directions I foresaw. Years later, many of them came back, stating that everything I saw did in fact happen, so they were ready to hear more. So, if people tell you that your visions are incorrect, know that sometimes only time will tell. Likewise, if you sense some future event for yourself and it doesn't happen when you thought it would, that doesn't mean that it or something similar won't still happen sometime in the future. The important factor is to learn to trust this ability and live your life more from its guidance.

One young lady was engaged to a man with blond hair. They had no desire to have children and they wanted to travel. To her dismay, I saw that if she remained on her current course—which she could because she had free will—she would be married to a man with dark hair and they would have two children. I also commented that I saw her living near a mountain. Years later, the woman returned. She had forgotten all about our session, but had recently stumbled upon the recording of that reading. She shared that her blond boyfriend had left her. She ended up marrying a wonderful man with dark hair, she had two beautiful children, and one day while washing dishes she looked out her window and realized they lived near a mountain. She was pleasantly surprised so was now back to hear more.

Of course, it's the people who receive accurate predictions that return. I have no way of knowing how many of the readings proved to be inaccurate since I have seen thousands and thousands of people. As you can imagine, disappointed people would have no reason to return for more. The majority of people do return, however, sometimes years or even decades later, declaring that what I foresaw came true. Either way, I continue to use my ability to read for people because it has created far more benefits than problems. I share this information with you to support you in also exploring and moving forward with your abilities, whether or not you are always right.

As you develop your own intuitive or psychic abilities, learn to trust what you're sensing even if people around you refute what you sense. Keep an open mind to be inaccurate, but also know that people are not always in touch with their own intuitions. Wishful thinking can override what their souls are telling them. Or they can choose to ignore their deeper gut feelings. Time will tell if you were picking up on something they were unaware of or in denial about. Or over time, you'll learn where you might have been projecting your own thoughts and assumptions rather than authentically hearing their souls. Either way, learn to practice your own abilities with no fear of failure. This is the best way to develop and grow.

Also, know that everyone gets to choose his or her own experiences. There really are no *right* or *wrong* paths, just *easier* or *tougher* paths. Even if you become very adept with these intuitive abilities and do your best to help people, they still have free will and will continue to make their own choices.

SELF-FULFILLING PROPHECIES

A case can be made for potentially creating self-fulfilling prophecies, which in and of itself reveals something amazing about the power of the mind. But with some of the following stories, you will see that self-fulfilling prophecies were not involved.

Two girls shared that their father's passing was imminent; the diagnosis they had received from their father's doctors was that he would die any day now. When I psychically connected remotely with their father, I heard from his soul that he would live three more years. That appeared to be impossible. The girls returned years later, reporting that their father had died exactly three years from the day we had our meeting. They never told their father about our conversation, so it couldn't be classified as a self-fulfilling prophecy. Rather it was information his soul knew and shared with us, and it proved to be accurate. Of course, our beliefs create our realities, but I'm not sure these girls actually believed their father would live three more years. So it must have been the father's soul that knew he would live longer than they expected.

Another very simple example involved a woman who called my radio show. I saw her taking a boat trip along a river in the Northeast soon to see the fall colors. I discovered later that after the show she commented to a friend that she had no plans to do that, so she believed I had picked up incorrect information. However, days after the show, family members who knew nothing of our conversation called her to say that they had booked a boat trip down a river in the Northeast to see the fall foliage. They wanted her to join them. She called the show again weeks later to share what had happened and to say that, even though she knew she had free will and could have declined their invitation, she thoroughly enjoyed the trip.

Many people declare that the insights that came through in their sessions were responsible for considerably changing their lives for the better. They moved to a nicer location, saved their marriage, or married an emotionally healthier person, shifted their health, changed to a better job, gained information that helped them understand their children and become better parents, and more. Again, I share this information to show that this ability can be used to help people.

You have these same intuitive or clairvoyant abilities. You don't have to become a professional psychic. I trust that you will find a way to use your own enhanced skills to benefit you and others.

What the Existence of These Abilities Reveals

The fact that many of us demonstrate these intuitive, telepathic, and psychic abilities shows that:

- **We don't have the boundaries or limitations we think we do. We have more extraordinary abilities than we've been taught.**

If I am accurately able to see exactly who has survived a plane crash before any search party has found them, or see that someone has a life-threatening health issue without even meeting him, then I'm not picking up information from their body language or by asking them a lot of leading questions. I'm also not researching them in advance on the Internet, as some people claim that psychics do.

Many others have had similar experiences, so we are proving that these abilities are real over and over again. Being "good guessers" cannot account for the many details authentic psychics can see. For example, my percentage of accuracy over the past three decades has gone way beyond any normal probability if I were relying only on chance; and the number of intelligent and professional people who continue to return for guidance and information reveals that something bigger is going on here.

- **Time must not be what we think it is.**

If I can see someone's past, present, and future, these must all exist now. That's the only explanation I can think of for why I can see them. If the future didn't exist now, I wouldn't be able to see it. So if time is an illusion, or not as one-directional as we've thought, what else can we do if we aren't limited by time?

If everything exists now, then our past doesn't cause our present. We are free to create our future and our past from this very moment. We no longer have to be traumatized or affected by the past. We create everything in our lives from this present moment.

"The present is the point of power."[5]
—JANE ROBERTS, *THE NATURE OF PERSONAL REALITY (A SETH BOOK)*

We can create in all directions. We can change our past from this present moment just as easily as we can create our futures. We've been taught that we cannot affect the past, that it has already happened, it's set in stone, and we can have no effect over it. But if time is an illusion, or if everything is happening simultaneously, then we have no directional limitations. Our past, present, and future can all be influenced by our thoughts and beliefs right now. (We'll explore this concept further in Chapter 7.)

Also, if time is an illusion, why would we ever "run out of time"?

THE SCIENCE

The principles of classical physics have dominated our thinking and perception of reality for hundreds of years, since the time of Isaac Newton (1642–1727).[6] We still believe in and operate within those principles, even though they are hundreds of years old.

The reason classical physics has ruled our lives for so long is that its principles have given us a very testable worldview of the universe. The principles appear to explain what we perceive with our five physical senses, so we have completely bought into this version of reality. But what if the following principles have been all wrong? And what if we've *created* this current version of reality because of these faulty assumptions?

Classical physics principles are:

- **The principle of space and time.** In other words, physical objects exist separately in space and time in such a way that they are localizable and countable, and physical processes (growth and evolution) take place in space and time.

- **The principle of causality.** In other words, every event has a cause.

- **The principle of determination.** In other words, every later state of an object or system is uniquely determined by any earlier state;

- **The principle of continuity.** In other words, all processes exhibiting a difference between the initial and the final state have to go through every intervening state; and finally

- **The principle of the conservation of energy.** In other words, the energy of a closed system can be transformed into various forms, but is never gained, lost, or destroyed.

Some of the assumptions of Newtonian physics are that:

- The brain generates consciousness and it is trapped inside our head.

- Physical matter is the only fundamental reality, and all processes and phenomena can be explained as manifestations or results of matter. This is materialism.

- We are separate bodies and cannot know about anyone or anything else unless they tell us or we gain information about them from an outer and tangible source.

- Time is real and only flows in one direction (forward), and we are limited by it. The future doesn't exist yet, and therefore it isn't possible that events can be seen or known ahead of time. They are not known until they occur in space and/or time.

Quantum physics, on the other hand, has evidence to support different concepts (the following two in particular), which may explain why these abilities are possible.

- *Non-locality:* Consciousness is not limited to the brain.

- *Quantum entanglement:* Once two particles have come together, they are forever bonded or connected no matter how far apart they may eventually travel from each other.

Let's first look at non-locality.

Non-Locality

Non-local mind reveals that consciousness is not limited to the brain; it exists beyond the brain and the body. It is also not bound by space or time. There are many physicists now who base their research on this concept. I will discuss this further and offer proof that non-local mind is real later in Chapter 8.

Scientists are probably going to debate whether or not non-local mind is real for some time. Many of us demonstrate non-local mind every day with telepathic and psychic abilities, so I trust some day science will catch up with people's experiences.

To help explain the concept of non-local mind vs. the idea that the brain generates consciousness, I use television broadcasting as an analogy. Inside a television set, there is a lot of activity involving electrical currents and circuits. This activity is similar to the electrical activity neuroscientists see in the brain. The programs you are watching on that TV, however, are not being created by that electrical activity inside the TV. The shows originate somewhere else; they are being broadcast from a network that transmits signals out in many different directions over the airwaves and your TV receiver picks up those signals. Those broadcasted waves are everywhere around you (like non-local mind.) The signals just become focused inside your TV so you can watch your show. It doesn't mean your TV creates those programs.

In a similar fashion, the brain (like the TV) does not generate consciousness. Your consciousness can be everywhere and anywhere, unbounded in time and space beyond your brain and your body. It is non-local. You are much more than your body, but you focus part of your consciousness inside, or as your physical body, just like the network signals are drawn inside your TV so you can experience the shows.

Because television signals are everywhere in the air, it's just as possible to have the same show appear on many different TV sets all over the city, without affecting or weakening the signal going to any of them. (We'll discuss these *parallel universes* or other TV sets later.)

We can also use computers as an analogy for non-local mind. Your computer does not generate the myriad of websites found on it, even though there are many circuits that light up inside the computer. The information and sites are created elsewhere and the signals are broadcast out into space. High-speed Internet signals are all around you, even though you can't physically see them (like non-local mind.)

The brain is like a computer. And something superior, our soul or our consciousness, operates the computer. Our soul uses the brain like we use computers. Science is at a loss to explain how the brain can translate electrical synapses into pictures or memories, so they avoid discussions about consciousness. Even if a scientist can stimulate a certain part of the brain and cause a person to move his arm, it still doesn't prove that the brain creates consciousness. Someone's consciousness (the scientist's) still stimulated that person's brain. *Stimulating* your computer (hitting a key or typing in a certain website) can bring up a letter or an actual website onto the screen. But the computer didn't do it by itself; a user (consciousness) stimulated the computer.

Even once scientists create artificial intelligence (possibly robots that can think for themselves), it doesn't mean matter generates consciousness. As we saw in the double-slit experiment, the subatomic particles that make up matter already appear to be aware since they react and change from a wave into a particle when someone is looking at them.

The concept of non-local mind can explain why *sensitives* (psychics) are able to pick up information about people who are somewhere else in the world. Our consciousness is not trapped inside our bodies and not limited to what our brains can see or hear at that moment. Our consciousness is free and can connect with other people's consciousness anywhere in the world—or even beyond this physical world.

Now let's look at another discovery from quantum physics that could explain why intuitive, telepathic, and psychic abilities are possible.

QUANTUM ENTANGLEMENT

This is another concept that supports these enhanced abilities. What quantum physics has discovered is that once two particles have come together they are always bonded or entangled, no matter how far apart from each other they might travel in space or time. If one entangled particle starts spinning, the other entangled particle starts spinning simultaneously.[7] No signal travels through time or space from one particle to the other; they both experience the effect at the exact same time—instantaneously. They seem to be instantly *aware* of what is happening to the other and respond accordingly.[8]

Particles have awareness? Apparently. This is another example that reveals that they might be aware. We explored this concept when we discussed how to create with energy.

Erwin Schrödinger coined the term *entanglement* to describe this peculiar connection between quantum systems. He said: "When two systems, of which we know the states by their respective representatives, enter into temporary physical interaction due to known forces between them, and when after a time of mutual influence the systems separate again, then they can no longer be described in the same way as before, viz. by endowing each of them with a representative of its own. I would not call that one but rather *the* characteristic trait of quantum mechanics, the one that enforces its entire departure from classical lines of thought. By the interaction the two representatives [the quantum states] have become entangled."[9]

Scientists attempt to explain our origins with the big bang theory, which states that everything came from a singularity, or a single point, and then suddenly exploded and expanded into what we now know as the visible universe. If science is correct that we did originate from the same place or source, then everything in the universe has always been entangled. We all were—and continue to be—connected. Therefore, it's not difficult to surmise why and how psychic abilities could be understood: One way is through entanglement.

Explorations of the quantum field also have shown that because everything is made of energy on the energetic level there are no real boundaries between one object and another. The fact that everything is connected on the energetic level also lends support to the case for psychic connection and being able to know about someone no matter how far apart we are from him or her in time or space.

Many of us legitimately experience the things that quantum physicists have been discovering and theorizing about for the last century. New discoveries in the field of physics are continuing to alter the way that we, including quantum physicists, now perceive reality.

✦

IF YOU WOULD LIKE TO LEARN ABOUT AN INTERESTING STUDY in consciousness, check out the Global Consciousness Project (see Resources section). This is an international, multidisciplinary collaboration of scientists who collect data continuously from a global network of physical random number generators located in seventy host sites around the world. The information gathered from each location is transmitted to a central archive, which at this writing contains more than twelve years of data. Their purpose is to examine subtle correlations that reflect the activity of consciousness in the world.

In lay terms, this group measures random number patterns generated by computers. Usually the computers generate random 0s and 1s. There is no pattern to when a 0 will be generated or a 1. Imagine a coin toss. A random number of heads or tails will show up during the tosses.

However, the researchers have graphs that show during intense or peak emotional experiences for masses of people, such as during natural disasters, the typically random results in the data are no longer typical or random. There are anomalous spikes in the data, which means that during these times many more 1s or 0s show up. If it were a coin toss, a significantly higher number of heads than normal would show up. Deviations like these occur whenever there is a widespread reaction to a major event.[10]

For example, the emotional response from millions of people that occurred when U.S. President Barack Obama gave his moving acceptance speech caused the readings on the graph to spike. They also find unusual readings on the graphs when there are massive natural disasters. And strangely, beginning a few hours *before* the first airplane hit the World Trade Center, the measurements on the graph started to show an uncharacteristic rise. It continued to rise, peaking when the Twin Towers were hit, and continuing during the emotional reaction around the world. The probability that this effect is due to chance is less than one in a billion.

The scientists in the Project are theorizing that a field of consciousness is involved in the results they are seeing. This means that we, as conscious beings, must collectively be much more aware of future events than we previously knew, otherwise it is improbable that the graph would have started rising *before* the Trade Center was actually hit.

SPIRITUALITY

Psychically connecting with people that I've never met, who live in different places around the world, and accurately knowing many details about them supports a case for quantum entanglement and non-local mind. It also corroborates many spiritual teachings.

For centuries, mystics and spiritual teachers in diverse cultures have touted the connection and wholeness of everything. If we're connected, if we're all One, then we have access to and knowledge of everyone and everything.

In Buddhism, the term *anatman* means that all things are interconnected and interdependent, so that no thing has a separate existence.

Physicist Fritjof Capra describes the parallels between modern physics and the ancient Eastern philosophies of Taoism, Hinduism, and Buddhism in his book *The Tao of Physics.* He compares the essence of modern physics to the teachings of the Chinese *Tao Te Ching,* the Indian Upanishads, and the

Buddhist Sutras. These philosophies agree that consciousness is related to the "ultimate reality," which physicists know as the quantum field.[11]

The book of 1 Corinthians 12:13 says: "For by one Spirit are we all baptized into one body, whether Jews or Gentiles, whether bond or free; and have been all made to drink into one Spirit."

People who have had near-death experiences frequently share that they are now aware we are all connected, parts of a grand field of energy or consciousness. They also describe that while they were out of their bodies, they were able to feel other people's emotions and knew what those people were thinking and saying, even if they were not in the same room.

We've heard this information before, but are we implementing this knowledge in our lives? Are we actually changing our lives when we learn that we are all connected? Or do we just continue on with our seemingly separate activities, worrying about our financial situations and fretting over our jobs? Most of us don't know how to apply this knowledge in a meaningful way because we haven't been taught that this is reality. Life is so much more spectacular than the small worries we currently focus on. Maybe all of us can now come together and start living this wisdom and new information about reality by using our greater abilities, those that validate our connection.

SKEPTICS AND CONCERNS

"Argue for your limitations, and sure enough, they're yours."[12]
—RICHARD BACH, *ILLUSIONS*

Some think psychics are kooks, new age space cadets, or delusional. Or they believe that psychics are charlatans who deceive unsuspecting people. While some self-proclaimed psychics do fit that stereotype and some are indeed fakes and charlatans, it doesn't mean that the people who are authentically using intuitive and psychic abilities are that way.

My definition of a psychic is someone who has developed expanded consciousness, someone who has actually activated the natural skills that we all have.

WE CAN'T . . .

Some believe psychic abilities aren't real, that they're not possible. It's probably easier for me to believe in these enhanced capabilities because I have been experiencing them since 1984. There will always be people who resist new ideas, who prefer their familiar versions of reality. The value of skeptics could be to provide us with choices. They offer options so we can choose what we want to believe. If everyone believed the same things, life would be boring. We would never know we had a choice to believe something else.

The belief in gravity is such a case. Most people believe in gravity. They consider it an absolute scientific fact and part of reality, so we haven't yet broken free from its hypnotic grip. And this holds true despite the fact scientists don't really understand what gravity is or why it is such a relatively weak force. Maybe having a different, less restrictive understanding of gravity would offer us more freedom in some way. Historically, each new discovery has led to more freedom.

Without mavericks, explorers, and people who question old beliefs, however, we might not ever break out of old patterns or outdated belief systems. There would be no one to poke holes in old paradigms or challenge existing strongholds, which means we would still believe in a flat world, one planet, and more. We're delving into other concepts and options that most don't know exist.

WE SHOULDN'T...

If you are someone who doesn't believe we should see the future, consider how many people are in professions that do involve predicting the future: doctors, weather forecasters, therapists, teachers, architects, pilots, parents, and many more. All of them see the future.

If your doctor saw that your weight was leading you to diabetes, or that your arteries were blocked and you were headed for a heart attack, and she didn't tell you, wouldn't you think that she was being negligent? If a weather forecaster saw a hurricane headed to an area and didn't warn the residents, that would be irresponsible. If a therapist saw that a patient had emotional issues and sensed he could do harm to himself or others, and did nothing about it—well, we've seen the atrocities that can occur from that scenario! Knowing you will be going to work on Monday or visiting family for the holidays is still a form of predicting or seeing into the future.

Maybe your protest isn't actually about seeing the future—because we all do that at some time. Is your concern about how one attains information about the future? If someone attains the information from research, hard work, or surmising something logically, rather than from a heightened intuition or from connecting with a greater Source, then it's okay? Many doctors and therapists, and even parents, will tell you they often have a *feeling* about a diagnosis or a situation that is not always based on logic, previous experience, or test results.

Where people draw the line about which predictive abilities and technologies are acceptable and which are not is very subjective and usually based on their personal beliefs of right and wrong. For my part, if the information helps someone, then I assume the ability is an asset.

CHAPTER FIVE

ENERGY FIELDS AND AURAS

"All truth passes through three stages. First, it is ridiculed. Second, it is violently opposed. Third, it is accepted as being self-evident."

—UNKNOWN AUTHOR, ATTRIBUTED TO ARTHUR SCHOPENHAUER (1788–1860), PHILOSOPHER

Not only are we made of energy, we also emanate energy and are broadcasting who we are all the time. Whether or not you realize it, you are able to sense this energy. Considering that everything is made of energy, why wouldn't we be able to perceive this energy? Many people do report seeing auras or radiating light around living things—plants, animals, and people. So if some of us are able to see and sense auras, all human beings must have that same capability.

Even if you haven't been able physically to see auras yet, you have most likely *felt* the radiating energy. It probably explains why you feel instantly comfortable with some people and uncomfortable standing near others. You're feeling their energy.

You can further develop this ability to see or sense energy if you desire.

I experience the aura as softly glowing light (like the light from a light bulb) that radiates out from, and surrounds the entire body. There are layers of different colored bands in the aura. For example, there may be a band of yellow light closest to your body with a band of blue light appearing next to the yellow band. Both bands encircle your entire body. Then there are multiple other-colored bands that show as layer upon layer in your aura. Each colored band reveals something different about you.

The energy that radiates from you is basically photons (particles of light) moving in the form of waves. The different colors are created by different frequencies or wavelengths of energy. There are no good or bad colors; they're just different.

This energy field has been scientifically detected through electronic equipment, such as Kirlian photography and gas discharge visualization (GDV) cameras.[1]

People may experience the aura differently. Various people see different colors or interpret each color differently. It doesn't mean someone is right and the other is wrong. We're just having different experiences, just as we taste and experience food differently. (Many people like lima beans, so I know they don't taste what I taste.) Some of us see the personality colors or life colors in the aura; others may see the colors that reveal the ever-changing emotional qualities of a person at that time. I encourage you to trust what you see and interpret what each color means to you.

In my experience, people have many different colored bands in their auras. The outer bands in your aura change all the time, depending on what is happening in your life at that time. For example, if you become angry red will show up in the outer bands of your aura. The one or two bands of color in your aura that are closest to your body, however, are your life colors. These bands of color typically do not change. The life colors reveal information about your personality, your life purpose, your relationship style and needs, your best careers, your strengths and your weaknesses concerning money, health, family, and much more.

The colors in your aura don't *control* your life; instead, they reveal who you are and the theme that you have chosen to experience in this lifetime. Some people have compatible auras and are able to get along more easily; while others can repel or irritate one another and it takes more effort to create harmony between them. Understanding the different aura color personalities could help us all get along.

We actually use the aura color descriptions in our language. We talk about someone being "true blue" or "feeling blue today." Those descriptions fit a Blue aura color personality. Obviously a person doesn't turn blue when they are being loyal or depressed, so where else could these sayings have come from? We use terms like "red with passion" or "red with rage," which often describes a Red aura color personality. A Red aura color personality is different than the temporary red that flares up in the outer bands when we are angry. We have yellow "happy faces" and the "yellow-bellied coward," which can describe the jovial, but oftentimes insecure Yellow aura personality. We have "green with envy" and green money, which are Green traits and interests. And the royal violet robes fit the regal Violet personality. So people somewhere must have seen the aura colors to use this particular terminology.

MY EXPERIENCES WITH AURAS

After a year of working as an intuitive, I met a woman, Barbara Bowers, Ph.D., who could see auras around people. I realized that the colors she was seeing in the energy fields and the personality traits she attributed to each color corresponded to the same personality qualities I was picking up psychically about people. After observing her work for a while, I also developed the ability to see and sense these energy fields, and to understand what the different colors revealed about them.

When I first began seeing auras, I only saw a subtle white glow that extended out about two or three inches from the person's head. I later discovered this is a common experience for people when they first start seeing auras. So this may be your first experience as well. A woman offered to help me further develop my ability by standing in front of a white wall and imagining bursts of energy coming out of the top of her head. I was pleasantly surprised to see the white light suddenly glow brighter and shoot up about a foot above the top of her head.

For months, I was only able to see white auras. Slowly I began detecting the colors. I didn't force it or try too hard; the colors just started appearing on their own. Understanding what each color meant in advance helped me learn to see the individual colors. I sensed the personality of the person, which helped me look for that corresponding color in the aura. That same technique may work for you, in which case you may want to study the personality type that goes with each color. I have listed some basic examples of each color personality. Understanding what each color reveals has been a helpful tool in my psychic work. It's been a good way to begin exploring a person's life purpose and life path.

Here are some brief descriptions of the different aura color personalities.

Physical colors: those who process information and life primarily through touch and their physical bodies.

- **Red:** physically passionate, sensual, strong willed, enjoys taking physical action (Madonna, Lady Gaga: Red with Magenta, Sean Penn, Russell Crowe, Marilyn Monroe)

- **Orange:** physical daredevils, thrill seekers, extreme athletes (Evel Knievel and Jackie Chan)

- **Magenta:** eccentric, outrageous, creative, loves to shock people (Andy Warhol, Liberace, the character of Kramer on *Seinfeld*)

- **Yellow:** fun loving, humorous, and youthful; artists, athletes, and healers (Johnny Depp, Brad Pitt: Yellow/Tan. Jennifer Aniston: Yellow/Violet/Blue)

Mental colors: those who process information and life primarily through the intellect.

- **Tan:** analytical, practical, values stability and security, usually works with details or technology (Clint Eastwood: Tan/Violet. Harrison Ford: Tan/Yellow. Tommy Lee Jones: Tan/Violet.)

- **Green:** driven, intelligent, business minded (Bill Gates, Barbara Walters, Mark Zuckerberg, David Letterman: Green/Yellow. Warren Buffet: Yellow/Green)

Emotional colors: those who process information and life primarily through their feelings, emotions, and inner senses.

- **Blue:** emotional, spiritual, supportive, teachers, counselors, relationship oriented (Ellen DeGeneres, Kaley Cuoco, Goldie Hawn: all Blue/Yellows. Elizabeth Taylor: Blue/Violet)

- **Violet:** visionary, leader, passionate about helping the masses (Oprah, George Clooney, Bono, Steven Spielberg, George Lucas, Martin Luther King, Jr., Nelson Mandela, the Dalai Lama, Gandhi: all Violet/Yellows)

- **Lavender:** daydreamers, creative, sensitive, imaginative (Lewis Carroll, C.S. Lewis: both partially Lavender)

- **Crystal:** healer, quiet, intelligent, spiritual, sensitive, easily overwhelmed (no celebrities known)

- **Indigo:** androgynous, spiritual, psychic (Michael Jackson: Indigo/Violet)

If you're interested in learning more about each aura color, I go into greater depth in my books *Life Colors* and *Love Colors*. Go to www.lifecolorscity.com.

A WOMAN WAS CONCERNED about her young daughter's intensely rebellious behavior. This client had beautiful Blue and Yellow aura life colors, which are typically the aura colors of loving and sensitive pleasers. These personalities want people to love them. They don't like to cause trouble and they shy away from conflict. When I tuned in to the woman's daughter, who was at school at the time, I discovered the daughter was a Violet/Yellow personality. Violets are huge personalities and love being the center of attention. They need to experience big and important lives, so they are usually powerful, outspoken leaders and performers.

Our lovely mother was trying to raise her daughter to be a sensitive, courteous, and thoughtful Blue/Yellow like herself. Her powerful Violet daughter was railing against what she felt to be her mom's suppressive and non-supportive behavior. When I explained the characteristics of Violets, their life purpose, and what they need to feel fulfilled, the mother shared how her daughter had verbally expressed those very same needs and desires. The loving Blue/Yellow mother had been overwhelmed and intimidated by her Violet daughter's powerful energy, which she interpreted as demanding, selfish, and out of control. The daughter had felt her mother wasn't really hearing what she had to say, nor understanding who she really was, so she became louder and more aggressive in an attempt to be seen and heard.

Violets, when they are balanced and emotionally healthy, are dynamic, inspirational visionaries with deep compassion and a grand destiny to live. They feel a need to inspire others, educate the masses, and improve the quality of life on the planet, even if they do this by performing. When Violets are frustrated, they can become indignant and dramatic tyrants. They can become spoiled, self-absorbed, out of control, and ungrateful. But more often when they are off balance, they experience fear—especially the fear that they won't accomplish their dreams. Many suppressed Violets can act like powerful eagles trying to claw their way out of a small birdcage. If they are suppressed long enough or not supported to live their bigger dreams, they can actually become lost and depressed. Critically depressed Violets often look for severe ways to end their pain. Most eagles don't survive living in captivity. Violets, like eagles, need the freedom to fly to their ultimate heights.

Once the mother understood the characteristics of Violets, the dynamics of her relationship with her daughter changed. The Violet daughter became much happier and their relationship vastly improved. The mother finally understood what her Violet daughter needed and began speaking her language. Together they explored appropriate Violet outlets and had frequent mature conversations. Violets are usually more advanced than their peers, so they need honest and direct communication.

This is just one example of the benefit of being able to sense and understand the different aura color personalities.

MOST OF THE EXPERIENCES I HAVE WITH SEEING AURAS involve knowing people's life purpose, most compatible life partner, and best career direction. So many people are in unfulfilling careers because they've been taught they should live as a different aura color personality. That causes them to suppress their natural desires and talents. A Violet/Yellow man was unhappy in his Tan job as a computer programmer, for instance, and then he finally found happiness in the more creative music business. Likewise, an easygoing, creative Yellow stopped experiencing severe health issues once he let go of his highly stressful Green position as a fast-paced financial broker—the field his successful Green CEO father had encouraged him to pursue.

Many couples are able to save their marriages once they discover each other's aura colors. It helps them realize each other's true needs and priorities, and learn each other's *language*. Once the nurturing Blue wife understood that her husband had a Tan aura, she learned to appreciate his stable and reliable behavior rather than become frustrated by his tendency to keep his feelings to himself.

More than one parent has relaxed once they discovered their unusual child was a psychic Indigo or the introverted Lavender. So many parents worry that there is something wrong with their atypical children and are unsure how to raise them, until they learn about each child's unique aura color personality. Lives improve once they learn what's important to that aura color and what parenting techniques are most effective.

Once you know your loved ones' aura colors, you can be supportive and bring the best out of them.

HOW TO SEE AURAS

We all came into this lifetime with the ability to see and sense energy fields or auras. Over the years, I've observed infants and animals reacting to the different aura colors around people so I'm assuming they see or sense auras, which leads me to believe we were born with this ability. Infants may be able to still see auras because they haven't been taught otherwise. A baby will often smile and reach out to one person and cry and pull back from another. I've seen the reason they may have acted this way when I notice the person's aura. I've also watched a dog bark at one person with a red overlay, yet befriend another with the childlike yellow aura. Observe babies and animals sometime to see if they look above the person's head. This is usually where the aura is the brightest.

EXERCISES

Different people sense and experience these radiating energy fields or auras differently. You may visually see the aura, or you may experience it physically, psychically, emotionally, or even intellectually. The method that works best for you may depend on your aura color personality. Use the method that feels natural to you and then trust what you experience.

If you haven't experienced sensing auras before, you may want to first use the same meditation and visualization process that we used for developing your intuition and psychic abilities in Chapter 4. This can help you shift into to a more expansive and relaxed state, which can help you become more receptive and sensitive to energy.

- **Exercise to feel the aura:**
  You may process life more kinesthetically than other people, and therefore first sense auras through your physical body. You may feel the energy or heat in the aura through your hands. Heat is radiating energy. Many healers have a natural ability to feel energy with their hands and can quickly move into feeling auras.

  In a relaxed and calm state, face the palms of your hands toward someone and hold them approximately three feet from that person's body. Then, slowly move toward the person until you feel the sensation of heat or energy. In the beginning, you may feel something when you are a few inches away from the body. However, with patience and practice your sensitivity can increase and you'll eventually learn to feel a person's aura from a greater distance. Most people have about six feet of differently colored, layered bands in their auras; while some more introverted people have auras that extend only about one or two feet from the body.

- **Exercise to see the aura:**
  When you first start seeing the aura, you may see a white or clear glow around a person's head. This is where the aura is typically the brightest.

  Have someone stand in front of a white background while you focus either on some part of the face, like the forehead or nose, or just above and past the person's head. Look with soft eyes—with the same relaxed focus you use when you daydream. You may see best with your peripheral vision, meaning you may notice a subtle glow around the person in a different area than where you are focused. Notice if you see a soft white glow around the person's head or body. If you change your gaze and look directly at it and the glow goes away, you have just experienced seeing an aura. Don't try too hard and don't stare directly at it. Struggling and trying hard will not work. Relax and just let the image come to you.

Many people assume that what they are seeing is an optical illusion, an afterimage of the physical body. For example, if you stare at something red for a while and then look away, the opposing color green may appear before your eyes. This is an optical illusion. To prove to yourself that you are seeing the aura, ask the person to concentrate her energy and imagine sending an intense beam of light out from the top of her head. You should be able to see the white glow around her head intensify or fluctuate.

You can also practice seeing the aura around your hand. Hold your hand in front of a white background and with a soft gaze look either just past it or in the center of your hand. Notice if you are able to see a white glow around your hand out of your peripheral vision.

It may take a while before you see the different colors in the aura. Colors may spontaneously appear at some point without you even trying. You can practice looking at the auras of different people to see if you notice any subtle differences in their auras. This may be a way to start realizing you are sensing the different colors. Some people find it useful to close their eyes and imagine the person who is standing in front of them; sometimes a color appears around the image. This may be the way you know the person's aura color. Your inner vision may intuitively know better than your outer eyes.

Or, as I stated before, the colors began appearing for me once I sensed the person's personality. I knew what a Blue personality felt like so I was eventually better able to sense the Blue in her aura. If you learn the personality descriptions of different aura colors and you are able to recognize someone's qualities, it may eventually help you see the aura colors. Of course this only works if your ability results in you seeing the same colors as I do.

When you do start seeing colors, know that different people can see the colors differently. There is not a correct way of seeing or interpreting the different colors. Trust what you see or sense and ask yourself what those colors mean to you.

Whether or not you see the colors, being able to see the aura can still be helpful. Even a white or clear aura can reveal the state of a person's physical health or emotional wellbeing.

THE BEST METHOD FOR YOUR AURA COLORS

If you are a **Blue, Crystal,** or **Lavender** aura personality, you will usually intuitively sense a person's energy field before you are able to physically see it. You can also sense whether the person is insecure, sad, happy, or angry just by becoming quiet and feeling the person's energy, even if that person has not exhibited any obvious outer signs in her behavior.

If you are a **Yellow, Red, Orange,** or **Magenta** aura personality, you will typically be highly kinesthetic. You process life predominantly through touch and your physical body, so you usually feel the aura through your hands or body first.

If you are a **Violet** aura personality, you are typically very visual. Violets tend to see the aura before most people do. Your third eye is usually highly developed.

If you are an **Indigo** aura personality, you are one of the most psychic people on the planet. Most Indigo souls have retained their ability to see and feel auras. However, you may find yourself accessing all of your abilities: psychic, clairvoyant, clairsentient, clairaudient, or more to sense auras.

If you are a **Tan** or **Green** aura personality, you can be highly analytical, so you will often do best when you first study all the different personality traits of each color, and then learn the different techniques to detect auras. Then relax and let go of trying to figure out how it works. Just allow the image to appear.

Remember to practice. It may take some time and more practice before you are able to start seeing or sensing the aura. Don't give up or get discouraged. We have learned everything we do by practicing. Just don't struggle with it or make it hard work. Relax and let it show itself to you.

You can practice on your own by looking for the auras around animals or plants. Use the same technique. Relax your gaze and with soft eyes look past the animal or the plant. Everything gives off energy. Notice if you see a white or clear glow around anything in your world.

Make sure you are not afraid to see auras, because that fear could hold you back. Are you concerned your friends and family will think you're crazy? Do you fear they will judge you? Are you afraid of your own power or intuitive abilities? You'll need to move past your anxiety if you are to successfully develop this or any other skill. Trust that these abilities can help you and others, that they won't harm anyone.

We are moving into a time where more and more people will become aware of energy fields. The ability to see auras is a natural one. We've just forgotten how to see them. It can be an easy skill to reawaken.

THE BENEFITS OF SEEING AURAS

Auras may reveal that we are, in fact, made of energy; or at least that there is a life force that animates us and radiates from us. If we can learn how to work with this energy, it could change how we see and interact with the *physical* world.

Learning to see and understand what is revealed in the aura could also improve the way we treat people with illnesses. We could diagnose and heal using energy and psychology rather than medications and surgery. Seeing auras can help identify or even predict health issues. If an aura is faded, for example, it indicates the person is very ill or about to die. When someone is deceased, there is no aura radiating from him or her.

Also, each aura color personality has specific potential health challenges. For example, the emotional Blues have a higher risk of throat, breast, and reproductive problems. The fun-loving Yellows have a tendency to have back, leg, knee, liver, and prostrate issues, and they are more prone to diabetes, which stems from a lack of joy. The driven, workaholic Greens often develop heart problems, ulcers, and other digestive issues. The visionary Violets often experience thyroid and vision problems. Knowing the tendency each personality has to develop specific health issues and learning how to prevent these issues from occurring can be a tremendous help to people.

Each color personality also has specific preventative actions they need to take to stay physically, mentally, and emotionally balanced and healthy. Prevention techniques that work for one color don't always work for another color personality type.

For example, if you are a Yellow aura color personality type, you usually stay healthy if you spend time in nature, exercise, eat healthy, get a massage, play, laugh, cheer up others, hang out with your dog, simplify your life, find reasons to be optimistic, smile, watch a funny movie, and laugh some more.

Green aura color personalities are very different than Yellows. If you are a Green, you feel best when you feel organized, in control of your life, and financially thriving. So it helps if you organize your space, reassess your goals and write a list of them, develop a plan, trust that you are competent, write a list of your past accomplishments, appreciate everything on that list, reduce your caffeine intake, and take deep breaths. Then, once you learn how to breathe, take action.

In order to stay balanced, if you are a Violet you will benefit most when you practice your favorite form of daily meditation, travel, listen to positive music and recordings of inspirational teachers, spend quiet time alone realigning with your visions, get involved with humanitarian projects, spend time with people who inspire and motivate you, and travel again—possibly to foreign countries.

You Blues tend to stay emotionally balanced and healthy when you pray, connect with a Greater Source, walk, breathe, meditate, spend time appreciating your home and loved ones, remember all the loving things you've done for others, let go of guilt, trust you are loved, learn to love yourself by also doing good things for you, learn to say no, help others without overdoing it, and spend time with supportive friends.

If you are a Tan, you feel healthiest and happiest when you take a break from focusing on so many details, rest your eyes, breathe, watch less news, read positive and optimistic information, exercise, develop a secure financial plan, find healthy outlets for your emotions, such as talking with a calm and rational friend who can give practical and trustworthy advice, and research any type of data that will make you feel more secure about your finances, the state of the economy and the world.

If you are an Indigo, your health improves when you meditate, pray, connect deeply with nature and a higher Source, write, create art, be quiet and listen inside, create a safe environment for yourself, develop a positive perspective of humankind, help animals or children, practice compassion, trust, and remember what your soul knows: that there is a reason for everything that is going on in the world, so it's best to be patient.

You sensitive and introspective Crystals need to meditate, pray, create a peaceful environment, spend quality time in solitude, read inspirational and intelligent books, breathe deeply, be with people you trust, listen to calming music, eat simple but healthy foods, be quiet, and spiritually reconnect.

You robust and physical Reds need to engage in hearty exercises, such as football, running, boxing, and martial arts. You also do best when you eat revitalizing and healthy foods, practice moderation and self-control, take physical action to help people (rebuild homes, rescue work, and so on), learn to manage your anger and frustration, and spend time outdoors.

In order to stay balanced and healthy, you Lavenders need to create a peaceful and calm environment, breathe, meditate, listen to soothing music, pray, simplify, spend quiet time in the serenity of nature, be with kind and supportive people, quietly daydream and imagine, and create art or music.

You outrageous and eccentric Magentas flourish best when you spend time around other unique and creative people, search for unusual items to create art, have fun at art galleries or thrift stores, entertain others, make people laugh, appreciate the absurdity of life, engage with people and life so you don't become isolated and depressed, do something rebellious that brings you pleasure, such as getting another tattoo, keep better hours (don't stay up all night), and eat healthier.

You daredevil Oranges are prone to injuries caused by your daring physical activities. So in order to stay healthy and uninjured it's best if you decide what adventure you want to do next, plan it carefully and thoroughly, figure out how to make the money you need to accomplish this venture, think creatively, and act intelligently and cautiously. Exercise, eat well so you're prepared for the task, get adequate sleep, learn to moderate and not overextend yourself, and then take action. Also consider getting involved in interesting and daring projects that also physically help people, such as rescue work.

THE BENEFITS OF KNOWING AURA COLORS

As you can see from the descriptions of each aura color personality, being able to see auras and understand the meaning behind each color can give you important insights into yourself and other people. It also gives all of us permission to be our authentic selves. This knowledge can help us all get along by allowing others to live their true nature rather than expect them to fit our expectations. We can learn to respect each other's language, needs, and priorities. Understanding and accepting each other can help us develop compassion and ultimately create a more peaceful world.

WHAT THE ABILITY TO SEE AURAS REVEALS

Being able to see and sense energy fields provides evidence that we are more than just our physical bodies; we don't end at our skins. It proves there is a life force that animates us and that we are not just biological machines.

And since the different aura colors reveal specific traits about people, it shows that we are broadcasting or sending out signals about who we are all the time. It may explain why we feel instantly comfortable with some people and uncomfortable with others. We're sensing who they are and whether or not they are compatible with our energy. Being able to feel or see auras also reveals that we are intuitive and able to detect more than we thought.

THE SCIENCE

So is there science behind these electromagnetic or biofields? In science, EEG and EKG machines work by measuring the electromagnetic signals from the brain and the heart respectively.[2] Some scientists believe signals from the rest of our body also carry information about us, especially about our health. Today there is scientific research being done on this human electromagnetic or subtle energy biofield (the aura) and what it reveals about a person's health.

An indicator that there has been interest in this area is that the National Institutes of Health funded research on human biofields.[3] Berkeley-trained biophysicist and founder of the Institute for Frontier Science Beverly Rubik, Ph.D., is one of the scientists conducting research on these fields. She believes that the human body exudes energy.[4] She also points out that when a person is deceased he or she no longer emits energy.

Harvard-trained psychologist Gary Schwartz, Ph.D., who runs the Human Energy Systems Lab at the University of Arizona, states that the existence of a human aura is indisputable.[5]

There are a number of people researching these biofields or electromagnetic fields. For more information, check out some of their research (see the Resources section).

AURA CAMERAS

If you have ever had a photo taken of your aura, the camera owners may have explained to you that the cameras measure your emotional energy at that time. Occasionally these cameras pick up a person's predominant life colors, but not always. Your emotional energy changes frequently, which is why the colors around you can change from one photo to the next. The life colors, by contrast, don't usually change; they reveal your personality and other such traits, which are fairly constant.

For anyone who doesn't know that these cameras detect the emotional frequencies in the aura rather than the life colors, it can be confusing to see orange in the photo and then read about the Orange life color in my book. That description will not fit that person's personality, because she is not an Orange life color. The person just had a lot of strong creative energy radiating off her that day, which the camera will show as orange.

When you get your aura photo taken, ask the camera operators to explain what those particular colors mean. It is a different system than the life colors system, but it can be just as helpful. To learn more about aura photography, see Resources.

SPIRITUALITY AND AURAS

Throughout the ages, artists have depicted the aura as a halo that appears around the heads or bodies of saints and spiritual masters. Apparently, the aura around these beings was so vibrant and powerful that others could easily see it.

Spiritual traditions teach that we are more than just our physical bodies. Most of the traditions believe that the soul has a purpose for being here. The purpose for this lifetime is revealed in the aura life colors.

YOU LEFT CLUES...

Through my experiences as a *sensitive,* this is the information I've learned from people's souls.

You chose this incarnation, this *physical* experience on the planet, and you had a good reason for doing so. You have free will, so you weren't forced to come here. You, as a soul or entity, are awesome, and deep inside you know exactly what you're doing, even if, like many of us, you have forgotten that. On a soul level, you are aware that you are completely connected with All That Is or Source.

You chose a certain theme for this lifetime. There are experiences you want to have, people you want to connect with, lessons you want to learn, or adventures you want to enjoy. You wanted to feel emotions—all of them—to taste food, see colors, smell flowers, hear birds sing and music play, fall in love, ride carousels, feel the earth, and more. You wanted to see what you could accomplish, contribute, or overcome. Are you remembering some of the reasons you came here yet? Maybe you forgot it was supposed to be fun and fascinating.

You left clues around you—just in case you came to this denser level of consciousness and forgot why you came. Forgetting seems to be easy to do on this plane. And we intentionally planned to forget so we could fully experience this life *movie.*

So you left clues or signs in many places to help you remember your life purpose and the theme you've chosen for this lifetime: your energy field (aura), your birth date and time (astrology), your hands (palmistry), your eyes (iridology), your name (numerology), and probably in more places than you remember right now. You can also depend on your intuition and your dreams to help you remember. Because your soul, which, again, is a part of a greater consciousness, really does remember why you're here and it speaks to you all the time.

If you study any of these systems, the specific information revealed about you in each should corroborate and validate the others. The information revealed in each system doesn't control your life, it reflects back to you what you have chosen and what you are currently choosing. While you may have selected a theme for this lifetime, you still have free will. Since you left so many reminders, however, it seems you really wanted to fulfill your life purpose and accomplish a particular plan.

If we're not enjoying life, it means we've forgotten who we really are. Life is about playing and creating. We didn't come here to suffer. And you don't have to unless you *believe* you do or unless your original plan was to struggle to overcome obstacles. And even then, you can change your original decision at any time.

Chapter Six

Parallel
Universes

*"'To fly as fast as thought, to anywhere that is,' he said, 'you must
begin by knowing that you have already arrived.'"*
—Richard Bach, *Jonathan Livingston Seagull*

There is more than one reality! I don't just mean that we
each have a different *experience* of reality. I mean there is
not just *one reality.*

What Are Parallel Universes?

Quantum physicists have evidence that there is not just one
universe; there are multiple universes. Together, these are
referred to as the *multiverse.*[1] Parallel universes are all around us.
They're like radio waves. We can't see them, but they exist. These
other universes are as close as your breath and they exist in the
same space as the universe you're in now.

An infinite number of other universes exist. And according to some quantum physicists, other versions of you exist in these other universes.[2] For every decision or choice you've ever made, there is one you that is focused in the universe that reveals the choice you did make; and another you that chose the other option. That other you, who split off into another universe, is experiencing a different life than yours and unaware of your existence in this universe.

I imagine this may be a challenging concept to accept. Most of us weren't taught about parallel universes and typically we don't perceive these other universes so this requires another leap in our understanding of *reality*. Our knowledge of the universe evolves all the time. For a long time, people didn't know that other planets or other galaxies existed, so it's not hard to imagine we haven't known about parallel universes until comparatively recently. Interest in the concept of the multiverse is growing stronger, however.

WHERE ARE THESE PARALLEL UNIVERSES? AND WHY CAN'T WE SEE THEM?

Radio waves can be used as an analogy to help us understand parallel universes. Radio stations are broadcasting all the time. We know that the radio signals they send out are around us everywhere—and yet we don't see them. We aren't experientially aware of their existence until we turn on a radio receiver and adjust the dial to the same frequency as a particular station's radio waves. If we set the dial to 99.9 FM, for example, the receiver aligns with the broadcast frequency of that specific station and we're able to hear the show they're broadcasting. That show then becomes part of our reality and experience.

If we change the dial to align with a different frequency, say 101.7 FM, we then hear the music being broadcast from that station. Now that program becomes part of our reality. The radio waves from the 99.9 station are still in the air all around us, but we no longer experience them as part of our reality.

In the same way, other universes are all around us, occupying the same space as our universe—literally as close as our breath. But we don't perceive these parallel universes because our mental and emotional frequency is aligned with the universe we're in now.

YOUR ABILITIES

What do parallel universes have to do with you and your life? Do you have the ability to intentionally change your life by aligning with one of these other parallel universes, one that may be a happier, more loving, or more prosperous universe? Or are the other universes something you'll never actually consciously experience and they'll be constantly out of your reach?

The answer is, *yes,* you absolutely have the ability to change your life by intentionally aligning with other universes. You shift into different universes all the time. You just assume there is only one universe so you're not aware that you've changed into a different one. You just focus on the one you believe exists. However, you do constantly and seamlessly flow from one parallel universe to another. Every time you choose one option over another, you shift into a different universe.[3] Another *you* will still exist in your previous universe, but because your focus won't be there you will no longer experience it as your main reality. Just like the previous station's radio waves are still around you when your dial is no longer tuned to them, but they're not part of your physical world.

There are an infinite number of universes where you are having completely different experiences—right now, simultaneously, and each unique universe has many diverse details. Some details may only vary a little between universes, while some of the details of your lives in other universes are radically different than in your current life. In a remarkable statement, physicist David Deutsch says that you could have actually died from an illness in one universe and still be very much alive in this one.[4]

Your choices could have been infinitesimally small at times. You could have chosen to wear a white shirt one day instead of a blue one, so in one universe you went off that day with a white shirt, while the other you in the blue shirt spent the day and every day afterward living a different life in another universe. The difference in your experiences could be so small and minute you would never notice being in a different universe if you happen to switch over.

You could have made a much more important choice, however, that significantly changed your life, such as marrying someone you met in high school. In this case, the version of you that made that choice could still be married to that person in another universe, while this particular version of you never married that person. Both have separate and individual lives of their own going on—simultaneously.

All of us have felt at some time that we made a choice that significantly changed the course of our lives. And we may wonder what would have happened if we had made a different choice. Well, there is another you that knows the answer to that question, and you can connect with that other you if you want to find out.

The people who are in your current universe will also be in the other parallel universes—they'll just be somewhat different. The differences in their behaviors could range from subtle to striking, depending on how radically you have changed your thinking. We are multidimensional beings so we all exist in an infinite number of universes simultaneously.

There are no visible seams or doorways dividing the different parallel universes, so it can be challenging to know when you have entered into a different universe. There are no visible walls dividing the different radio frequencies either; they coexist in the same air all around us. It is like driving from one state to another. Unless you see a sign that welcomes you to the new state, you don't always know when you've actually crossed the boundary line because the landscape is similar. Remember, some of the different parallel universes only have subtle differences from the one you currently find yourself. But if you pay attention, even if there are only subtle differences in the new universe, your intuition and feelings can reveal these differences to you.

Because there are parallel universes and infinite multiple realities, many different versions of Earth also exist. According to quantum physics, there is likely a version of the world where the British won the American Revolution, and a version where the Cuban Missile Crisis didn't end well and the world has been devastated by a nuclear war.

If some people envision the world coming to a catastrophic end, they could create that experience for themselves and therefore be in a universe where an end does occur. For those who focus on peace and believe that the Earth and its inhabitants will evolve, survive, or even thrive, they will experience that version of events. In the Bible, it is written, "The meek shall inherit the Earth."[5] The original meaning of the word *meek* was "peace loving," not the timid definition it has today. The point is: Your beliefs create your reality.

The existence of parallel universes reveals how we don't just move forward in one straight, sequential timeline. We actually exist and move expansively in all directions in all times in many dimensions—right now. This is what was meant by the comment made at the beginning of the book that some physicists have theorized that time may go backward and forward—*and sideways*.

The idea that you exist in parallel universes gives a whole new understanding of you as an infinite being, doesn't it?

If you would like to see visual or theatrical examples of how parallel universes work, some visionaries have created films based on this concept. The movies *Somewhere in Time* and *Frequency* are both about parallel universes. They show how making different choices significantly changes realities. *It's a Wonderful Life* is also about parallel universes, as are *Back to the Future, Sliding Doors, The Family Man,* and countless others.

I know parallel universes are real because I experience them. And in this chapter I will describe how you can use parallel universes to significantly change your life. I'll also share my personal experiences, revealing the steps I took to intentionally change universes and how this improved my life. Which universe you find yourself in is determined by your beliefs and your choices. You can change your life circumstances considerably by learning how to move into different universes. I did—and I continue to do so.

EXPERIENCES

The following is my most dramatic personal example of changing universes. Years ago, I had a strong desire to be in a relationship with a certain musician. He, however, wasn't interested in me. He stated emphatically that he wasn't attracted to me, wasn't in love with me, and never would be. Not long after that, he moved to the other side of the country to join a friend's band, assuring me he would never return. To say that I was devastated would be an understatement. I couldn't figure out why I could feel so strongly about him if we weren't going to be together. I struggled with the pain of this man's rejection for almost two years.

Then I found a segment on parallel universes in one of my Seth books, *Seth Speaks.* The Seth series of books profoundly changed my life and transformed my beliefs about reality. In these books, Seth explains how our thoughts and beliefs create our reality and that we have no limitations.[6] Those books began my exploration into expanded consciousness and parallel universes.

Reading *Seth Speaks*, I realized I believed I was unlovable and that love would never work out for me. I saw that I was aligned with negative images and so existed in a universe that reflected those beliefs. I knew I had to change my unhealthy beliefs about myself. I knew my thoughts affected my emotions and my emotions carried a frequency, and also that by changing my frequency I would align with a different, parallel universe. My strongest priority became changing universes.

One day, fully committed to change, I sat quietly in a meditative state for hours—a length of time I now realize was unnecessary. Change can happen in a moment. The intensity of the feelings is what causes the shift. At that time, I knew that my limiting beliefs had a strong hold on me, so I had committed that entire day to intensely focusing on transformation.

I sat quietly. I'll also mention that at that time, many of my girlfriends were in the same situation. They were also bemoaning their loneliness.

I felt that I was unloved and alone in Universe 1. (I'm numbering the universes to help describe the process.) In Universe 1, I assumed my friend was on the East Coast, happily playing in a band and being with a girlfriend. My feelings in Universe 1 were unhappiness, shame, and hopelessness.

Then, I imagined a thin veil hanging nearby in Universe 1. I moved toward this veil, parted it, and stepped through to Universe 2. I looked around, but this new one didn't quite feel perfect. In this universe, I felt my friend was with a different band and he wasn't with a girl, but I still felt personal feelings of inadequacy. I also felt guilty because of my desire to pull him away from his chosen life. So I knew I hadn't sufficiently changed my beliefs. I moved on to a different veil and a different universe.

I went through the process three more times, parting and stepping through veils into different universes. Each time, I saw diverse situations and environments. In each of the universes, my friend was playing with other bands and living a variety of circumstances. I am a very visual person, so these images helped me believe I was actually in different universes.

The following is a very important part of this process. When I left each universe, I had to completely step out of each one. I had to fully drop each undesired universe and not be attached to any part of it. I had to focus my full attention on the new one, believing it now to be my one and only, true universe.

When I eventually arrived in Universe 5, I observed my environment. I felt good in this one. I sensed in this universe that my friend did love me; he missed me and wanted to come back home to Santa Barbara. I completely immersed myself in this universe. I felt him with me, holding me and loving me completely. I felt lovable and worthy, not because he said so, but because I am lovable—as we all are. I felt my self-worth increase.

In Universe 5, I watched my friend give notice to his band and break up with the girl he was seeing because they weren't right for each other. They were both fine though—no one was suffering. I didn't feel selfish or guilty with this version. I saw him traveling to Iowa to see his meditating friends, then on to Los Angeles to see his musician friends. Then he would be returning to Santa Barbara. The scenes felt very real. I had a deep sense that this was all really happening in this particular universe.

For over an hour, I allowed myself to fully experience the colors, sounds, and sensations in Universe 5. I breathed everything in, felt the sun on my body, and enjoyed all of it. I felt happy in Universe 5, and that feeling stayed with me even when I stopped the meditation. I knew I was now living in a different universe. That is the key. You can't just hope you changed universes. You have to know you have actually shifted into a different universe.

My friend and I hadn't really spoken during the two years he lived on the East Coast. I hadn't known where he was. But two weeks after my meditation experience, I discovered where he was and called him. Why wouldn't I call him since I knew I was in a universe where he cared about me and would enjoy communicating with me? He told me that exactly two weeks earlier he had given notice to his band and had broken up with a girl, and they were both fine with it. He was on his way to Iowa, then to Los Angeles to see his friends . . . and then he planned to come back to Santa Barbara. Shortly after his return, we began a wonderful relationship. Like all couples, we experienced both joys and challenges. But we were a loving and committed couple for the next twenty-six years. And we continue to this day to deeply love and support each other.

Some may judge this story, imagining I *stalked* this poor guy or that I manipulated and controlled him—none of which I did. I didn't have to change, control, or manipulate him. In fact, switching universes had nothing to do with him. I changed myself. I changed my thoughts, beliefs, and feelings about myself, as well as my beliefs about the nature of reality. This person still exists in Universe 1, as well as Universes 2, 3, and 4, and an infinite number of others. I just shifted my focus and aligned with the universe where we were a loving couple. I aligned with Universe 5.

This person has free will and can focus on any universe he desires. Like me—and you—he exists in an infinite number of universes—some with me, some without me, some where we've never met, and some he continues to live on the East Coast. We all have free will.

Since I exist in an infinite number of universes, and in each one I am having unique experiences, that means that in some of these other universes, I could be married to past boyfriends and living in other locations. I could change my beliefs and my focus and experience myself in any one of them. I would just have to *completely believe* they were real. In my experiment, I chose to focus my attention on one of the universes where my friend and I both loved each other and wanted to be together. I could choose to focus on and align with a different universe at any time, with no fear. This is a playful universe with infinite creative potential.

We haven't been taught that this is reality, so this concept can be challenging for people to accept and implement.

An unusual side effect occurred when I focused on Universe 5, a side effect that proves to me something profound happened and it wasn't just my imagination. As soon as I moved into Universe 5, the one where I believed in love, happiness, and partnership, all of my girlfriends, who previously had been single and lonely in Universe 1, were suddenly in loving relationships. A few of them were even happily engaged! It felt as if no time had passed, but now in Universe 5 they were in happy relationships. In Universe 5, my friends were also optimistic and believed in love.

I wanted to be able to go to all of my friends and tell them that in Universe 1 they were unhappy and single. But at that time, many years ago, I was concerned they would think I was crazy, so I kept the information to myself. Now I'm sharing this incredible technique of switching to parallel universes with others so that everyone can benefit from this process.

When I shift my focus to a parallel universe, I continue to have all my friends and family in the new universe as well. They may be slightly altered. They may be happier. I have changed many unhealthy relationships this way. I stopped perceiving someone as a problem. I shifted my beliefs about that person and found myself in a universe where that person was different. Again, I didn't control or manipulate anyone. I changed me. I changed my beliefs, and then my outer world changed.

I realize this concept sounds like science fiction, but quantum physicists have evidence that parallel universes are real. And if they are real, we must be able to experience them.

THIS ISN'T THE ONLY TIME I HAVE USED THIS APPROACH TO LIFE. Years ago, I thought that having a radio show might be a good way to share empowering information with people. So I briefly imagined myself in a universe where I had a show. A few days later, I received a call from a friend at a station asking if I would be interested in having my own radio show. Weeks later, I was on the air!

This type of thinking flies in the face of old beliefs, the ones that tell us life doesn't work this way, that we must work hard, sacrifice, and be patient. And even if we do all of those things, there is still no guarantee we will get what we want. The United States has at its foundation, in the Declaration of Independence, "The right to life, liberty, and the *pursuit* of happiness."[7] Not the right to happiness, just the right to *pursue* happiness. So we have millions of people living in a universe where they are pursuing happiness because they believe that is the way life works.

I still occasionally slip back into old ways of thinking. I know how to shift my thinking and bring myself into a life-enhancing universe. But sometimes I find myself once again in a challenging universe. I know at that point to reexamine my beliefs and shift my focus so I can move into an easier, more pleasant universe.

If and when I do find myself in a challenging situation, I now realize that sometimes I am creating it just for the adventure, to see what I can overcome. Other times, I've just forgotten to stay aware of my thoughts and beliefs so I've unintentionally shifted into a struggle or fear-based universe. At that point, I observe my choices and either change my beliefs or go along with them for the ride.

I'm not saying that once you grasp the concept of parallel universes you will never experience struggles in your life again. We really are adventurous souls and sometimes find challenges interesting. I am giving you a tool so you can shift your universe when you are not happy with the one you are in. We are not victims; we are creators. We have free will and have been given the gift to create our own reality. We live in particular universes because of our thoughts, beliefs, and emotions.

Remember, you don't need to overcome or battle with anything to change universes. You actually need to stop feeding energy to any particular universe by struggling with it. You just step out of it and into another universe. Relax and play with this process. If you are working hard to change things, it shows you are still attached to a particular universe. You're still giving that one your energy and attention.

David Deutsch admits the idea of parallel universe takes some getting used to, especially when one consider what it means to our every day lives. For starters, it solves once and for all the ancient debate of whether or not we have free will. "The bottom line is that the universe is open," says Deutsch. "In the relevant sense of the word, we have free will."[8]

HOW TO CHANGE UNIVERSES

We shift into parallel universes constantly, but we aren't aware we're doing so because, up to this point anyway, we have believed there is only one universe and only one reality. We don't usually feel a gap in our experience when we shift, so we think we've just been in one universe all along, that there has been one steady forward flow in time with only one past.

To consciously change universes, you first need to accept that other universes do exist and it's possible to shift into any of them. You live in and experience the one you believe is real. Right now, you're focused in this universe: the only one you believe exists. If you believe in a different one, you can experience it. But you have to wholeheartedly believe in it and focus your entire attention on that one. Remember, you don't need to work hard or struggle to overcome your current circumstances. You just need to stop focusing on what you're experiencing now and focus on a different experience. You use your imagination and emotions to align with that different universe.

Every possible scenario that has ever been imagined actually exists. Everything you've ever desired already exists in parallel universes. So you don't have to work hard to create something. You just need to align with a universe where it is already yours.

It's not that you actually move into or *travel* into other universes, because you already exist in all of the different universes all at the same time, right here, right now. Just as the different radio waves exist around you right now, you don't need to travel to change radio frequencies. You just change the station; you change the frequency. In a similar way, you can align with your desired universe and its frequency if you want to experience that one.

When the frequency of your feelings is aligned with the frequency of a certain universe, you'll find yourself in that universe. The universe where you are unhappy and nothing ever works out for you may feel heavy and dense. The universe where everything is fun will feel light and easy.

Imagine being in a different universe and immerse yourself in the feelings of being in that universe. The frequency or energy of those feelings will draw you into that other universe.

Changing feelings or emotions like anxiety, sadness, depression, frustration, or anger can be challenging if you've become addicted to them. Emotions can seem to take on their own life. But it is possible to get out of their grip. You just need to take charge, even though at times it doesn't feel that you have the strength to do so. It may take commitment and determination, but if you shift your thoughts, inner pictures, and feelings, the payoff is worth it: You'll shift to a universe that matches the new frequency—to the universe you desire.

If you can't seem to make a substantial leap in your thoughts, imagination and emotions to change universes, then gradually adjust the dial on your thinking. In the past, when changing frequencies on a radio, you had to turn a dial and move through every frequency. You went from 101.1 to 101.2 and then to 101.3, and continued moving further up the dial. Now we can just push a button to jump instantly from 101 to 107.8. If you can't seem to make a big leap from one universe to another, just shift your beliefs a little at a time to move you to universes that are similar to the one you're currently in, and then just keep adjusting your thinking until you are actually in the universe you desire.

For example, if you can't make the leap from believing you don't have any money to believing you have extreme wealth, just imagine whatever does feel possible. Slowly adjust your mental and emotional "dial" to a better image nearby your current reality. Can you believe you could get a raise or that you have more money in your checking account than you thought? Do those pictures feel realistic to you? Or if you feel lonely and hopeless and can't seem to make the leap to suddenly believing you are happily married, can you at least shift to believing that you are a good person who has done loving things for others and that some of them love and appreciate you? Even small shifts in your imagination and energy can help you move into different universes.

You can take a series of small steps rather than big leaps in your beliefs. Once you get better at knowing this is how life works, then you can take bigger leaps and shift dramatically. You can eventually learn to leap from one reality to another as easily as pushing buttons on your radio.

If you make radical changes in your beliefs, your new universe will also appear drastically different. If you go back to thinking and feeling the way you did in the previous universe, you will be drawn back into that old one again or you'll think you never changed universes at all. If you commit to new thoughts and beliefs, you will eventually notice you've moved into a parallel universe. By the way, when you change universes, your past also adjusts itself to reflect that new universe.

I suspect that when we sense déjà vu, when we have the uncanny feeling that we've done something before, it's because we've connected with another self in a parallel universe who has had or is currently having that same experience, but perhaps only one second ahead of us. Since most experiences of déjà vu have a positive feeling to them, it's possible this means another you is sending you a message and reassuring you that you are headed in a good direction.

IF YOU FIND IT DIFFICULT TO BELIEVE you could literally *become* another you in another universe, know that you can at least *communicate* with another you in a different universe. You can obtain knowledge and skills from another version of you. There are no boundaries between you and your other selves. Some physicists question this idea. But if we explore the idea of being able to communicate with your other selves, you'll see that there is evidence to show that this could be true.

Your past self is still you, it's just not the exact *you* that is here today. Similarly, a future you is still you, it's just not the exact you who is sitting here today. When you have a memory, that could be a past you communicating with you. Or if you have a premonition or vision of your life in the future, that could be a future you communicating with you. This may be evidence that other versions of you do communicate with you.

One way you can benefit from communicating with other versions of you is if another you in a parallel universe learned to become a marvelous artist, but in this universe you didn't study art at all, you can telepathically obtain knowledge from that other you and suddenly have the ability to become a successful artist in this universe. This can be a useful way to utilize parallel universes.

Parallel universes could also explain where sudden bursts of insight come from. Many musicians report that they woke up one day with an original song flowing through their minds. (Paul

McCartney shared that the song "Yesterday" came to him in a dream.)[9] The songs may have come from other embodiments of these musicians in other universes.

Sometimes you *unknowingly* connect with another you in a different universe and have sudden insights. If you want to connect intentionally with another you in a parallel universe, the following exercise could help you do so. This exercise is designed to help you align with and move into a different universe. But if you prefer to remain in this current universe and just receive information from another version of you, you can use the same visualization technique to talk with that other you while you physically remain in this universe.

EXERCISE

This guided visualization is designed to help you actually shift into a different universe by stimulating your imagination and evoking different feelings and emotions in you. This shifts your energetic frequency. You already constantly shift into different universes, but usually you do so unconsciously. This is to help you consciously shift whenever you desire change.

It's important to believe that parallel universes exist or you'll think this exercise only occurs in your imagination. Keep an open mind. Consider that both quantum physicists and spiritual teachers say that other universes and unseen realms are real.

Relax and be playful. Enjoy the experience of shifting into parallel universes. I encourage you to practice as often as you can until it becomes natural and easy for you. If during this process you feel doubt or resistance, just keep going and see if you can alter those feelings. Breathe and smile along the way. You may want to do the process again and again until you experience a sense of certainty.

This exercise is just one way to shift into other universes. Once you realize that they really do exist, you can use whatever technique or visualization works best for you. It's easy. You breathe, know that it's real, use your imagination, and *feel* yourself in a different universe. Imagination and feelings are the keys. You can use this process as often as you wish.

Step 1. Relax.
Be open minded and allow yourself to experience life in a more expansive way. Take a deep breath and relax your entire body. Allow this to be easy. You're safe. The divisions between universes are actually invisible, but when you do this exercise, you'll envision some form of physical veil or curtain of light between them to help you know when you've shifted into different universes. Take a few deep breaths, relax, and enjoy the journey.

Step 2. Use your imagination.
Imagine standing in a beautiful meadow with the sun gently warming your body. As far as you can see, there are green, rolling hills covered with small yellow flowers. A soft breeze moves quietly over the green hills.

Just over to the side, you see a beautiful waterfall of light. Walk over to it, then gently reach out and touch this soft waterfall of light. It's so gentle. It sparkles when you touch it. It's safe.

Gently part this thin waterfall of light, like you're easily pulling sheer curtains apart. Before you step through, look back at the universe you're about to leave. There's nothing you need to do with this one, no obstacles you need to overcome, no one you need to fix, and no need to struggle any more. You don't need to be attached to this one any longer. All the things you see here exist because of past choices. It's okay to let them go now. You learned and you grew. Now, you're no longer stuck with this particular universe. The same people you know now will be in the new universe—everything will just be different. It's okay to change your life now, and to have a better life.

So just let go of this old universe now. Don't give it any more of your attention. Turn your attention to the new one. Step through the parted waterfall of light into the new universe. It's easy. Just step through.

We're experimenting right now. We're playing and moving into different universes. So look around at this new environment. This universe is not that much different. It looks and feels a lot like the one you just left. There are only slight differences. All the same people and some of the same situations are in this one, too. It's beautiful here, but we want to explore more, so we're going to move into yet another universe.

There's another lovely waterfall of light just over to the side. This one is even more stunning. It sparkles and shimmers. Let's move closer to it, so we can really see its breathtaking beauty. As you take a deep, calming breath, reach out and touch this waterfall of light. Feel it caressing your skin gently. It's so warm and light and soft. Gently part this veil of light—and then easily step through.

Look around. You're in a wonderful new universe now. This universe is just as real as the last two you just stepped out of. What is going to change in this universe is you. You are going to allow yourself to be your full greatness, to be confident and fully alive. Feel that aliveness in your body, feel the emotional energy of it. You can now live with love and joy and ease. You don't need to suppress who you really are any more. You can finally do what you're here to do. You're free to be completely authentic, to be your true splendid self.

Your true self is loving and full of joy. And because you now realize that you're much more wonderful and expansive than you thought, everything will come easily to you here.

Love and wealth and happiness and perfect health will all flow in abundance to you. You're safe to be you. Here, the real you is loved and accepted.

By living your true greatness, you'll be able to call forth anything in this universe. Universal energy loves to take form so anything you desire you can just call it to you and this energy will delight in becoming that. Everything you could ever desire is yours in this universe. It's all so easy.

Because you're completely happy here, your body is also radiantly healthy. Feel a warm radiant glow everywhere in your body. You can relax in that warmth. You're loved unconditionally and are completely healthy. This is your natural state of being. This is how you were created. Every cell in your body is alive and happy and ready for any adventures you want to have.

It's so beautiful here. The colors are vibrant and bright. Nature is so alive. Breathe in and feel the true immenseness of life.

Everyone you know is also here—though they're different from your prior universe. This universe is so easy and filled with love that they're all happy here. You can choose to spend time with anyone you'd like. They are all enjoying their experiences here, so you don't have to spend time with anyone unless you want to. They're already happy. You no longer have to rescue or help anyone. Everyone is fantastic here.

You're an adventurous soul, so you can stay here as long as you want. You can play and laugh and have fun—or you can explore any of the other universes at any time. They are there for you to enjoy. Everyone is playing in the different universes, just for fun, just to experience new things. The universes are playgrounds where we can all create different adventures. Most people create drama at some point along their life journeys. Some may do that to see how strong they are and what they are capable of overcoming, while others may do so just to see what the experience feels like. Everyone gets to explore and create any experience he or she desires. So as you encounter others who are experimenting with their adventures, allow them to have their experiences without trying to step in and manage their lives for them or to "fix" them. You can be compassionate, but allow them to make their own choices.

As you journey through your life, remember who you are and how you can move in and out of different universes. You're a loving, powerful soul who is having adventures. Imagine new circumstances in a different universe and easily move into that one whenever you want.

If you ever find yourself unconsciously slipping into a universe you don't like, one with struggle or unhappiness, that's okay. Unless you *want* to experience those things, just to see what they feel like, don't worry. You don't need to struggle or suffer or stay in a difficult universe. Just quietly lift your attention off that one and shift your focus onto a different one. It's easy. Just relax and breathe. Use your imagination and see yourself in a new beautiful universe.

You can easily shift into any universe now that you know they exist. You're actually in a different universe now than when we started this process. Trust that this new one is real. Notice as you go about your new life which things around you look and feel different.

Step 3. Return to being alert.
Take a deep breath. Feel your body—your very alive and healthy body. Breathe. Welcome to your new universe.

That was easy.
As you become more familiar with changing universes, you will eventually be able to just energetically slide into a different universe without having to imagine veils or waterfalls of light.

THE BENEFITS OF PARALLEL UNIVERSES

You are an infinite being with access to many creative tools. If you are adept at using your thoughts and pure energy to create your desires, then that ability alone is sufficient to change your world. If, however, you feel your current circumstances are overwhelming and too much to overcome, then understanding how to shift into parallel universes is another effective tool for you to use. You don't have to work hard to overcome anything. You just drop your current universe and step into a different one.

Being aware that there are other universes and intentionally choosing certain universes instead of unconsciously staying stuck in an undesirable one can appreciably improve your life. Once you learn how important your thoughts, emotions, and beliefs are in determining which universe you end up in, you can teach yourself to have dominion over them. The true laws of creation are easy. Notice how nature creates effortlessly. You can learn to live consciously by understanding and using these natural laws rather than continuing to struggle with your old, limiting beliefs.

THE SCIENCE

What is the science behind parallel universes and how did physicists first discover their existence? Science discovered that light is both a particle and a wave. In physicist Thomas Young's well-documented "double-slit experiment" he discovered that a single particle does not just occupy one position, as was previously believed. It can exist in many places simultaneously. On the quantum level objects are blurred, nothing is solid and particles can exist in multiple locations at once.[10]

When single particles of light, or photons, are shot one at a time through a single vertical slit in a partition and land on a screen that is some distance behind the partition, the image that develops on the screen on the other side of that partition is a single, vertical and uniform band of light where the photons have hit.

In the double-slit experiment, if a second slit is opened parallel to the first on the partition and single particles of light are shot through each slit, one at a time, the image on the screen on the other side of the partition changes in an unexpected way. One would expect the image to be two separate straight lines where the light hits the screen. But instead of the expected two separate lines of light, the light particles now form an *interference pattern,* a pattern of multiple alternating bright and dark parallel lines. This is a pattern that one would expect to see if waves (like waves of water) were sent through the two slits, rather than single photons.

When light waves (or you can imagine waves of water if that's easier for you) emerge from two slits in a partition, overlapping wave crests intensify and meet at the screen to produce the bright lines of light. Also, crests and troughs cancel each other out to produce dark lines on the screen because no light reaches the screen. The interference pattern is understandable if waves are sent through the slits because they interfere with each other on the other side. But single photons shot through one at a time shouldn't logically interfere with each other on the other side of the partition.

Physicists have deduced that each photon somehow spreads out and becomes a wave before it travels through the slits, which means it is in multiple places simultaneously. Then, as a wave, it goes through the two different slits at the same time and interferes with itself as if it is now multiple waves on the other side, creating the interference pattern.

The same mysterious result holds not just for photons, but also for other particles, such as electrons. Each particle seems to exist everywhere, in many different places at once—like a blur or wave spread out everywhere. This phenomenon is known as *superposition.*

However, particles only act this way when no one is looking!

A strange phenomenon occurs if detectors are placed at each slit to see what is actually happening, or if someone watches to see when an individual photon becomes a wave and goes through both slits at the same time. When there are detectors present, they register a single photon traveling through only one of the slits, never through both at the same time. So as soon as someone tries to observe a particle changing into a wave, or going into superposition, the photon somehow stabilizes into a single position, as if it knows it is being watched. The photons seem to be aware.

This is a fascinating phenomenon! Once more, consciousness is creating or affecting reality.

Some physicists believe the very act of our observation causes all the possible states of a particle to *collapse* into a single particle in a single position. However, Hugh Everett, who in his 1957 Princeton doctoral thesis first presented the concept of parallel universes in his "many worlds" theory, argues that the particles don't collapse into one position. He said this only seems to happen from our limited perspective.[11] He asserted that all the quantum states are equally real and that each version of a photon continues its own existence though we in our limited perception only see one result of the experiment.[12] We only see one photon, but other versions of us in parallel universes see all the remaining possibilities. Other versions of us see each of the other positions the photon took.

Some physicists conclude that there is no way to measure an objective reality because the observer (consciousness) always has an effect on the outcome of the experiment.

Classical physicists try to explain this strange phenomenon by claiming that the laws of quantum theory only apply to the subatomic world. But quantum physicists, such as David Deutsch, argue that the theory's laws must hold at every level of reality.

Deutsch says, "Because everything in the world, including ourselves, is made of these particles and because quantum physics has proven infallible in every conceivable experiment, the same weird quantum rules must apply to us. We, too, must exist in many states at once, even if we don't realize it."[13]

He also says, "All possible events, all conceivable variations on our lives, must exist. We live not in a single universe but in a vast and rich multiverse."[14]

SPIRITUALITY

Various spiritual traditions teach there are many levels or realms beyond this one. They explain that these different levels can be reached through spiritual growth and evolution, or that people can find themselves in different realms once they have crossed over. These different levels or realms could also be considered different universes.

We've been taught that we can't see these other realms. The concept of heaven is that it exists somewhere far away and we have no access to it until our soul leaves the body. Existing in another realm after you cross over, however, is comparable to being in a parallel universe. It's a similar, if not the exact same phenomenon.

When I speak to people who have crossed over, these beings basically exist in another realm. We just can't physically see them because they are vibrating at a different frequency, much like the radio waves that are around us. They exist in the same space that we do though. Our current concepts of both space and time are limited and incomplete. Time and space exist simultaneously and we are infinite Beings: meaning, we have no limits!

Actually on the other side, time has no meaning and souls experience space differently than they did when they were in physical form. Souls there report being able to "travel" by using thought. They can imagine being somewhere and they're instantly there, without having to move through time or space.

With our current beliefs about the "physical" world, the root assumptions of time and space still have a hypnotic hold on us. Hopefully, understanding parallel universes can help us begin to step outside of our perceived limitations and move beyond thinking we are limited by time and space. Perhaps we can learn from souls in these other realms, or other universes, that it doesn't have to take time for us to have what we desire, that what we desire already exists and is available to us now. And that space doesn't separate us from what we desire either. We are already connected with it and we just need to align with it and accept that it is already ours.

CHAPTER SEVEN

OTHER LIVES

"Quantum physics thus reveals a basic oneness of the universe."
—ERWIN SCHRÖDINGER

There are no boundaries or limitations to what you can do once you begin accessing your infinite, expanded abilities.

YOUR ABILITIES

Consciousness has no limitations. We only experience the limitations we believe are real. So once you know what is possible, you have the ability to see your other lives, which are often called "past lives," just as easily as you can see this life.

The reason we're discussing other lives after parallel universes is because there is a connection. Time is simultaneous: Past, present, and future all exist concurrently. This applies to all time—even other centuries and eras. I know this because many of us are able to see them all now. This is also why I refer to these lives as other lives rather than as past lives.

People who have had near-death experiences have also shared their revelations around this subject. While they were out of their bodies, some people became aware that all their other lives were still happening, simultaneously, right then. In spirit, there is no such thing as time.

In our traditional programming, we have been trained to experience time as linear, one moment at a time, in sequence, one after another. But some contemporary quantum physicists are questioning this assumption. We have greater mobility in the three-dimensional world than we would in a two-dimensional world: We can go up and down, backwards and forwards, and side to side. So physicists question why it is assumed that in the fourth dimension, time can only go in one direction: forward. Quantum physicists now accept the possibility of time travel, so we know that something has changed regarding their perception of the presumably linear, sequential, and forward-only movement of time.

The fact that people have other lives is harder for me to prove than some of the other things I have shown evidence for in this book, so I will share just a few of my many experiences and then offer names of experts who have done actual research on the phenomenon of other lives. If you want to examine this phenomenon further, you can read their research papers, articles, and books. There is strong, documented evidence to show that other lives are real.

EXPERIENCES

I gave a private session to a client in her home. While tuning in, I suddenly received an entire panoramic vision of her in another life. In this vision, she was living in Salem, Massachusetts, with her husband and daughter. I *knew* that her husband in that lifetime was her brother in this current lifetime, and that her daughter in that lifetime was also her daughter in this lifetime. I also picked up her daughter's name in that other lifetime.

I saw clearly that in that other life, the woman was accused of being a witch, then persecuted and killed. (I realize that may sound like a cliché of a past-life impression, but it's what I saw. And it has been the *only* occasion in three decades of doing this work that I have seen someone in that particular location and time period.) Before her hands were bound and she was thrown into a river to drown, the persecutors, who assumed that her husband and daughter were also witches, forced the woman first to watch her daughter and husband suffer the same fate.

As the reading progressed, the woman's face turned from pale to ashen white. Once the session was over, she grabbed my hand and pulled me into her study. There on her bookshelf was book after book on the Salem witch trials. She shared how she had been obsessed with the trials since she was a very young child. She also had a persistent and unexplainable fear that her daughter was going to drown. She felt terror any time her daughter was near any body of water, even a small puddle or a bathtub. To add an interesting twist to this story, her daughter's name in Salem was also her daughter's name in this lifetime. I had heard the name and shared it with her in the reading. She had never mentioned her daughter's name to me prior to, or during that session.

Years later, the woman reported that after our session she never again experienced fear that her daughter would drown. She realized where her *irrational* fear had originated and was no longer anxious that it would happen in this lifetime.

IN MY VERY FIRST ENCOUNTER WITH A SOUL ON THE OTHER SIDE, I had my eyes closed in an altered state when the image of a male appeared. This man looked like something right out of Greek mythology: bare chest, bulging muscles, loincloth, and all. This occurred early in my intuitive development, so I wasn't expecting to see a soul from the other side, let alone someone like this. I saw the man very clearly in my inner vision. He announced that we had worked together in Delphi in ancient times and continued to share information with me about that era.

I suddenly experienced waves of memories. I had a full vision of being an oracle in ancient Delphi. I saw vivid images and knew many details about what had happened to me in that lifetime. Up to that point, I knew nothing about that era or that town, although I had always felt drawn to large, white pillars and Greek architecture. My home is decorated in a similar white Mediterranean style.

Years later, I watched a documentary on the oracles of Delphi. They stated, and therefore confirmed for me, many of the things I knew about that time in history. I also knew they were incorrect about some of the theories they shared on the program. For instance, I knew the oracles didn't have psychic hallucinations because of toxic fumes that were arising inside the caves. I also knew that oracles didn't babble nonsensically and needed a priest to interpret their messages for them. The oracles were clear communicators on their own. Later in the program, the narrator made similar comments. By the end of the film, the historians ultimately admitted it was just a theory they had about the gases being the cause of the oracles' predictive abilities; they didn't know that for sure.

While I had no scientific proof that I was (or am) an oracle in Delphi, I know it unquestionably. And to me it explains why I am proficient with clairvoyant abilities in this lifetime.

HOW TO SEE OTHER LIVES

Sensing other lives can be one of the trickiest abilities to develop. When you tap into *the field* and connect with scenes from other lives, it can feel like your imagination is working overtime. It can also be one of the most challenging processes to verify. You can ultimately verify the information that arises from intuitive abilities and psychic predictions, you can see the results of using energy to manifest things, and you can also see the changes in your world when you shift into different parallel universes. But unless you can see or hear actual names, dates, and other specific details during your visions of other lives, it can be challenging to prove what you are seeing. Most of the time, you'll need to rely on your intuitive sense to confirm for you that whatever you're seeing and experiencing is real.

It's rare for people to have been someone famous, which would make it easier to verify the facts. It can also be challenging to hear precise names and dates of non-famous people in a "past-life regression" session so that you can research and verify those details in official records—although it can be done. Many people have been able to recall exact names and locations of their other lives. Psychiatrist Brian Weiss, M.D., and others have been able to regress people under hypnosis and then locate those names and other data in official documents.[1] It's often easier to have a professional regress you to get details. However, once you fully develop your enhanced skills, you can easily access your other lives on your own.

Whether or not you work with a professional regression therapist, it's best that you learn to rely on your own feelings about your other lives. You are the best judge of whether or not a vision of another life feels authentic to you.

Exercise

You can find a past-life regression therapist who is adept at guiding people into other lives. But if you don't have access to someone like that, this guided exercise could help you have a similar experience. Just commit to the process and allow the information to emerge. Don't project ideas or force visions. Just allow yourself to see what shows itself to you. You may want to ask your higher self or a higher power to give you clear visions of your other lives.

The key to experiencing other lives is learning to quiet your mind. If you have developed the ability to go into deep meditation, this process may be much easier for you.

Begin in a safe and quiet environment, a place where you will be uninterrupted. Make yourself comfortable. Make sure you are not hungry or thirsty, and ensure you do not have any other physical needs. Also make sure that all your phones are turned off and other distractions are out of your environment (pets, kids, and other people).

Be fully committed to accessing this information. Clear intention can be one of your best tools. And since other lives are similar to parallel universes, you can use a similar process to access them. If you enjoyed your journey of going into parallel universes, you can also use that same exercise to go into other lives (see Chapter 6, "Parallel Universes").

Take deep breaths and relax. Take your time. Feel calm and safe in this quiet space. Each time you breathe, relax even more. Feeling calm and relaxed before you proceed with this process is essential because otherwise you could project your thoughts into a scene rather than actually experience your other lives.

When you're ready, imagine yourself in a quiet and beautiful environment. Open land stretches out far and wide in all directions. See a long, broad path in front of you. Completely relaxed, begin walking down that path. You notice many different beautiful waterfalls of light everywhere around you. Each waterfall is a different exquisite color with light that sparkles and flows, like a sheer veil of silk.

Notice one of the beautiful waterfalls of light that attracts your attention. Walk over to that one and gently part it like it is a simple veil. It feels warm and soft to the touch. Easily step through this waterfall to see what's on the other side.

As you step through, you enter into one of your other lives. You can see the vivid colors, hear the sounds, and even smell the air in this environment. You realize where you are, the time and the place. You also easily sense who you are in this lifetime. What century or time period is this? Look at your body and see what you look like. How you are dressed? What do you do in this life? Where do you live? Look around and see anything that is important to you in this other lifetime.

Off in the distance, you see people that you know. Notice who they are. Do you know any of them from this life? You see one of them turn and smile at you. That friendly person walks over to you and says your name very clearly. Notice what other details you see or hear here.

Breathe and relax. This is easy. Enjoy your time here right now.

Take your time looking around and observing everything you can. See if there is anything or anyone you feel a connection with in this lifetime. Remember any important information that can help you. See if anyone here has anything important to tell you.

Relax and walk around in this world for a while. Enjoy your time here. Look around and notice everything. How does this lifetime feel? You can stay here for as long as you want.

When you are ready to move on, turn and walk back to that same waterfall of light. Take a deep breath. Smile. Then, easily walk back through the waterfall and into this current lifetime.

Look around at your current world. It's wonderful here, even better than you imagined.

You now know a lot of information from that other life. You can return to that path at any time and walk through any of different waterfalls of light any time you'd like. Behind each waterfall is another lifetime to explore.

You can also do this exercise with friends. You can take turns guiding each other through the process to see what's on the other side of your different waterfalls.

THE BENEFITS OF KNOWING OTHER LIVES

The best reason to develop your ability to know about other lives is to recognize that you are a much grander being than you've realized. You are actually an unlimited and eternal being. You are adventurous and curious, and you're having many experiences in many different places and times. You are continuously discovering, creating, and evolving.

Learning about different lifetimes has helped people release unexplained and often debilitating phobias. Traditional therapies are sometimes unable to discover the root of people's issues. Using hypnosis and past-life regression to uncover the deeper causes behind certain behaviors has become more and more accepted, and has often been more successful at resolving such issues than the traditional approaches. For example, the woman with the other life in Salem who was afraid that her daughter would drown hadn't been able to cure her persistent anxiety about this until she finally learned where her fears originated.

Discovering that you also have relationships with specific people in other lifetimes can help you understand why you may have certain feelings about them in this lifetime. Many people report feeling an instant connection with someone they've just met, a familiarity, as if they have known each other before. There is often an instant love or easy rapport. This goes beyond the psychological explanation that the person reminds them of a friend or family member.

This sense of *knowing* someone can also be negative, however. People can feel an instant and reactive dislike toward someone they've just met. One of the benefits of accessing other lives is being able to explain these types of feelings. At least once you are aware that the unexplainable negative feeling may be because of another life, you have the option to heal or release that feeling.

In addition, because other lives are happening simultaneously, if an unpleasant situation is occurring between you and that person in another life, you can resolve it by healing it in this life. In other words, what you do and learn in this life affects all your other lives. Lifetimes are not sequential. You are not being punished for something you did in a past life, since all those other lives are still happening now. You have free will to affect all those lives here and now. If you are happy, loving, and empowered now, all your other lives will also benefit from that energy. Conversely, if you are lonely or unhappy in this life, you can connect with your other selves for guidance and support to help improve this life.

OTHER STORIES

Many articles have been written and shows produced about a woman named Jenny Cockell, a member of Mensa (the high IQ society), who lives in the United Kingdom.[2] From the time she was four years old, she was bothered by reoccurring visions of being an Irishwoman named Mary, who had eight children. Her visions became so strong and so persistent that she finally decided she had to see if she could find Mary's children and resolve the issue.

In her visions, Jenny repeatedly saw a town, so she drew a map of it. Not only did she eventually find this town, she discovered her name had been Mary Sutton, born in 1897. But before she went to track down Mary's children, many of whom she discovered were still alive, she shared her detailed visions with a BBC researcher. She wanted to make sure that the facts would finally confirm her visions and memories. She shared exact details about the family home, how it was built, what was in the house, the pictures on the wall, and even the kind of sewing thread that Mary had used. She even had a vivid detailed memory of the children catching a live rabbit in a trap.

When she found the site where her home had been in that other lifetime, all that was left was rubble. She did find the surviving children and they corroborated all the details of her visions. Apparently this woman was so distraught about dying and leaving her children that her soul wanted to return to make sure they were fine. (Yes, this appears to be a linear "past-life" story. But remember, we currently still believe in and therefore experience time as linear and sequential, so her story and experience while she is in a physical body would come across in a linear and sequential way.) You can read about Jenny's experience in her book *Journeys Through Time*.

FROM THE DAY HE COULD TALK, Cameron Macaulay remembered and shared many important details of another life: his name in that lifetime, his father's name (Shane Robertson), where his family lived on the island of Barra off the coast of Scotland, what their house looked like, how planes used to land on the small beach in front of the house, how his father died, and more.[3] After years of hearing about these details, his parents finally acquiesced and took the boy to the place he often spoke about and found *everything* he had described.

THE LATE IAN STEVENSON, M.D., was the former head of the Department of Psychiatry at the University of Virginia School of Medicine, where he was the founder and director of the Division of Perceptual Studies. Stevenson spent the last forty years of his life scientifically documenting over 3,000 cases of the past-life memories of children from all over the world.[4] Many scholars admit that these cases provide compelling evidence of reincarnation—or as we know them in the framework of this book, other lives.

Through these 3,000 case studies, Dr. Stevenson discovered common denominators. Children usually begin talking about their other-life memories between the ages of two and four.[5] They talk about their previous life with intensity and feeling, as if it is still happening.[6] Often they can't tell which life is real now (more evidence that our other lives exist now, and not in the past). These children can experience a kind of double existence where at times one life is more prominent, and at times the other life takes over. This is why they usually speak of a past life in the present tense, talking about their parents from another lifetime as if they were in this present life.[7] Almost all of these children are able to remember the events leading up to their deaths.

These other-life memories gradually dwindle when the child is between the ages of four and seven. Some continue to remember their other lives well beyond this age, but they stop talking about their memories for various reasons, including the fear of being ridiculed.[8]

SPIRITUALITY AND OTHER LIVES

Many cultures believe in *past* lives and reincarnation. And many spiritual teachings mention reincarnation, Buddhism being one of the more well known. Even the Bible mentions reincarnation. Jesus tells the disciples that Elijah reincarnated as John the Baptist.[9] We are eternal beings. *Eternal* means being without beginning or end, existing outside of time, infinite, boundless, and timeless. We have always been.

> *"Before you were formed in the womb, I knew you."*
> — JEREMIAH 1:5

Do you remember ever not existing? Most likely you don't remember being in the womb or being born; and you probably don't remember being one month old. So it's not hard to imagine that most of us also don't consciously remember where we were before we were born into this lifetime either.

PLAYS

To help us understand how other lives work, imagine that you're in a theatrical play and all the people in the performance are playing different characters. You connect with each other in the production, interacting and playing various roles in a saga that has a certain plot or storyline. Then, when the play is over, you go backstage for a while to hang out with the other actors, who now have become your good friends because you've all performed in this piece together.

Sometime later, you decide to participate in another play. You choose an interesting plot, write the script (leaving room for spontaneity and improvisation), and begin acting in this play. Each actor pretends to be a different character in this new piece.

You pretend that you don't know each other so that this new performance can be convincing. You're now different characters, living different storylines, and you're all very convincing performers in your roles. Although sometimes when you meet one of these actors in the new play, you do have the feeling that you've known this person before. He seems familiar, but you don't know why. . . .

Now you do.

Some of your actor friends join you in the new play. Others decide to be in a different performance this time around. But you know those actors will join you again in another play at another time—if they're interested in the plot, setting, era, and theme of that other play.

You may decide not to act in a play for a while, choosing to take a break between plays instead. So you hang out backstage or go home for a while, until you're ready to be in another production. That's taking a break between lives.

We're very creative souls and love to create plays, movies, and other adventures. So once you decide you want to create another performance, you once again choose the setting, theme, and other details. Then you gather up actors who want to be in the same drama, comedy, or action adventure and agree on what roles you're going to play in this new production.

It's no accident that the Renaissance happened when it did: Many creative souls wanted a similar artistic experience at that particular time. Similarly, certain souls were attracted to the theme of the Industrial Revolution, while others were drawn to the challenges of the two World Wars. Each soul wanted to have specific experiences or overcome particular challenges. If you question why souls would choose these types of experiences, notice how different people are drawn to various types of movies. Some enjoy romantic comedies, while others prefer dramas, action films, or horror movies. It's fascinating what types of plays we choose to create and to participate in just for fun or to learn something, or to see how that particular experience feels.

Doing psychic readings for decades and speaking with many people who have crossed over, learning how to use our thoughts and beliefs to create our reality, and having playful adventures is what life here on Earth seems to be about. Ultimately you won't forget the other actors because you have an infinite connection and bond with them.

Sometimes, certain actors don't enjoy working with one another, so they don't perform in more plays together. However, speaking in linear terms, I have discovered that when certain actors have issues with each other, they'll often choose to keep doing plays together until they resolve those issues. Just a thought for those of you who think that once someone you dislike dies, you're done for good. If you don't want to perform in a sequel together, you may want to resolve your issues in this lifetime. People typically don't like shows that end with loose ends, they want to complete the story. If an issue of yours isn't resolved, then your soul may voluntarily create a sequel to end the play and the relationship in a different way.

This idea has troubled a few people in the past, so let me restate that you have free will. You don't *have to* return with that person—or even to return at all. It will always be your choice. Just remember, most people don't like stories that are unresolved or that leave you hanging.

It's often the case that someone who is *challenging* you in this lifetime is doing so because on a soul level he or she loves you very much. This person has chosen to play the nemesis for you in this lifetime to help you learn something that you wanted to learn or experience something that you wanted to experience.

Now add to this analogy that all these different versions of you are participating in plays that are happening simultaneously and you can see what a multidimensional, multitasking being you really are.

CHAPTER EIGHT

TALKING TO THE OTHER SIDE

"The world that you know is a reflection of an inner reality."
—JANE ROBERTS, *SETH SPEAKS*

W e are infinite beings and our lives continue throughout multiple lifetimes. We also exist outside of physical incarnations. One of the reasons I know this is because many of us have had numerous conversations with people who have crossed over. And we have strong evidence validating that it is in fact those particular souls who are communicating with us. They still exist. They are just in other realms, vibrating at a different frequency.

YOUR ABILITIES

You have the ability to communicate with people in different realms who have crossed over to the other side. We only experience apparent separation because we believe in it. We've either been taught that when people die they cease to exist, or that souls go to a realm that is beyond our reach. You may have already felt your loved ones around you, however, so you may sense there is more to the story. Trust what you feel.

Some people believe we can't connect with departed souls, while others teach we shouldn't connect with them. I support us going beyond our old limiting beliefs. My experience is that the people who have crossed over want to connect with loved ones here. Some souls in the other realms show up to reassure their loved ones that they are happy, surrounded by family, no longer in pain, and in a place of peace and joy. Some show up to offer support and guidance to their friends and family. Some give details of their passing, often because the official details were not known or to give comfort to family members who fear they may have suffered during their crossing.

EXPERIENCES

I'm sharing how I do this process and what I do to access people on the other side in case my explanations help you understand the process. These same steps may also work for you. If nothing else, maybe my experiences will show you that these abilities are possible. Later, I will share an exercise to help you shift into an altered state of consciousness, which can make it easier to access the other side.

IN DECEMBER 2011, I RECEIVED A CALL FROM A CLIENT. Two young men were missing in the Mohave Desert. This client was there with one of the boy's mothers, who was desperately searching along with the search party. I quieted my mind and asked my client to describe the hair color and eye color of one of the boys so I could focus on him. Then I concentrated on that boy only. This is how I usually pick up a signal on a person. By quietly focusing on the boy, I soon felt an energetic connection with him.

As I connected with the young man, I was drawn to him, as if something was pulling me to where he was. I felt as if I was in a ravine with him. I had a full conversation with him in my mind, listening to everything he said and seeing everything he described. Then, I began seeing visual images in my mind of what the boys had been doing. I just allowed the images to flow to me; I didn't force anything to happen. I saw the boys racing an all-terrain vehicle up and down the mountains in the dark. The "movie" I saw in my mind revealed which one had been driving and what their current terrain looked like. I mentally asked how far away from the town they were and sensed that they were not that far away from their hotel. I also heard a mileage number pop into my mind.

To get a sense of which direction the boys were, I asked my client, who was still on the phone, to face north so I could use her as a compass. Then, I calmly focused on her and felt myself become her. I sensed which direction I needed to turn to go to the boys (southwest of the town). She listed the names of all the different mountain ranges in the area. There were so many of them, I was worried that I would get it wrong. Plus, so many people were out hunting for the boys and projecting so many different images that it became even more confusing. Everyone had a different idea and picture of where the boys were and I sensed many of their projections. I had to continuously clear my mind and become very quiet to distinguish which pictures I was picking up and which images others were projecting. Finally, when she mentioned the name of one particular mountain range I felt a subtle sensation in my body.

The signals of intuition can be subtle, but when you're quiet, you can feel something say yes when the right answer appears.

The search party was more focused on the area southeast of the town. The leaders were thinking the boys might have gone into one of the old abandoned mines. In reality, the search plane had already flown over the ravine where the boys were, but the terrain was such that the accident was difficult to spot from the air.

In the meantime, I made an energetic connection with the other boy. The second boy had shown himself to me without me trying to connect. I just saw a picture of him in my mind and knew I was now speaking to both boys. They spoke telepathically to me: in other words, I could hear their thoughts in my head. They showed me images of the ravine. We had a mental conversation together as if we were old friends.

Their bodies were eventually found right where they had shown me: the direction, the distance, the mountain range, the ravine, and other details. Unfortunately, at that time the official search party was not taking advice from a psychic. Fortunately, but sadly for their families, they eventually found the boys anyway.

One interesting aspect of this incident is that I was having a conversation with young men who had died and were no longer in their bodies, and therefore had no brain activity. This confirms to me that it's not our brains that generate our consciousness. Who we are is not contained or limited to the body.

Actually, it wasn't apparent to me while it was happening that these boys were no longer in their bodies, because they were talking with me as if they were still in the ravine. Because consciousness still lives on and people can continue to communicate, it can be challenging sometimes to know if people are still alive and in their physical bodies, or have left their bodies and crossed over to the other side.

A WOMAN IN HER SIXTIES ARRIVED IN MY OFFICE. She appeared calm and rational. There was no indication of anything unusual about her, except that her aura was faded. That is an indication that someone is about to leave the body. The person is about to die.

I did the same process of quieting my mind, focusing on her, and energetically feeling myself connect with her. When I finally made a connection with her, I discovered she was so unhappy that she was suicidal. I continued to listen inside to find out why. In my mind's eye I could see the image of an older man standing next to her. To describe what this is like, it begins with a sense that someone invisible is standing there. (Don't worry. It's not a scary feeling.) Then an image forms in my mind and I can sense the person's appearance. I don't see a strong physical form or an outline of a person. It's an inner knowing that this is what the person is like. I also get a sense of the person's personality. When you do this process, just allow images to come to you. Don't struggle or try too hard. Just trust you'll see or hear something in your mind.

Take a moment and describe your mother's appearance and personality out loud right now. Actually do this: Pause and describe her right now . . . Where did you go in your mind to get an image of her? Maybe you projected an image of her standing in front of you, or you had a vision of her being in her home when you described her. How would you explain to someone where your consciousness was or where you were focusing your attention when you imagined her? This is the same challenge I face when I try to explain how I see someone on the other side. It's almost as if you go into a "thought realm" to see the person you're describing.

Back to the older gentleman standing by the client. He telepathically told me (thoughts emerged in my head) that he was her husband. When I asked if she had recently lost her husband, she burst into tears. The man informed me that he had taken his own life. The woman was distraught because he hadn't left a note, so she had no idea why he had killed himself. She blamed herself and felt she could no longer live with the guilt and emotional pain. She had come to me as a last resort.

The information her husband shared with me was that he had just been diagnosed with Alzheimer's disease. He had valued his mind and intelligence above all else. His self-worth was tied to his sharp intellect and his ability to be successful in business. He shared that he couldn't bear the thought of losing his mind. At that point in the session, the man apologized to his grief-stricken wife and encouraged her to paint, travel, and spend time with their grandchildren, as they had planned to do together.

At the end of the session, the woman commented that she had received enough detailed and accurate information to reassure her that it was indeed her husband who was speaking to me. I watched as her aura regained its radiance. She had decided to live, to continue moving forward with the plans she and her husband had discussed, even if she would be doing so without him.

This story shows how those who have transitioned can still participate and influence the lives of their loved ones here. In this case, the man saved his wife's life from the other side.

A FRIEND CAME TO ME ONE DAY IN DESPERATION. His mother had slipped into a coma and her doctors reported that she would never come out of that state; she was too ill ever to recover. Since only close family members were allowed in the hospital room with her, he asked me to tune in to her remotely to see if there was anything they could do for her.

When I psychically connected with my friend's mother, she transmitted images to me. I saw her sitting on a bench in a beautiful park. This is the peaceful vision she was imagining for herself. I envisioned sitting down next to her so we could chat.

She told me she wasn't going to die; she just needed some time away from everything to contemplate her life. I told my friend what she said, that she wasn't ready to die.

For an entire month, my friend's mother and I had many telepathic conversations while she remained in a coma. Each session she told me what she wanted, and every time the family confirmed that these requests were her typical behavior. During our first few sessions together, I experienced an uncomfortable feeling, a lump in my throat. It was tough for me to swallow whenever I connected with her. I discovered later that she had tubes down her throat. Once I found that out, I was able to adjust my connection with her and let that feeling go. So know that you have control over what you feel. You don't have to suffer, even if the person you connect with is suffering. You can release any type of physical or emotional feelings.

Over a month later, this woman finally emerged from her coma—just like she said she would. And contrary to the doctors' prognosis, she lived another eighteen years. The fact that she did survive the coma, and that she shared with me her plans to do so prior to regaining consciousness, shows that something outside of our traditional medical understanding is happening. The woman supposedly had no functioning activity in the area of the brain that is responsible for communication and awareness, so again, this shows me that it's not the brain that generates consciousness.

SOULS OF PEOPLE WHO HAVE CROSSED OVER usually give detailed personal information to prove to their loved ones that it is, indeed, them speaking to me. Often they use specific words or mannerisms that can help their family members recognize them. I frequently find myself using hand gestures or facial expressions that are not my own familiar gestures; they are, however, the same ones formerly used by the departed loved ones.

Sometimes these souls give unusual details unknown to their loved ones, such as where their family can find missing documents, heirlooms, hidden money, and more. And the relatives do invariably find the items where they have been told to look. This is not information known to the relatives and hence it's not a case of reading minds or being psychic. Rather it is about speaking to the departed souls and hearing what they have to say. Here are two examples.

Two sisters had searched their father's home for days looking for important insurance papers. From the other side, their father directed them to a particular desk drawer in his exercise room in the basement, a place they hadn't even thought of searching. That is exactly where they found the documents. This is another case of someone helping his family from the other side.

A deceased uncle directed his young nephew where to find a buried tin can that was filled with cash. This is not a common message, since most people don't bury money in their backyards. The young nephew did find the hidden cash right where he was told to look.

How to Connect

People often ask me what I see, hear, and experience when I communicate with souls on the other side. What I experience varies with each person. I often feel their presence first; then I see them with my inner eye. I sense their personality, hear in my mind what they want to share with their loved ones, and sometimes see movies of their lives. I share these details with their family members so they can confirm it is indeed their loved one.

In a similar way, when you connect with people on the other side, you may first sense their presence. If you sense their physical appearance, most souls will purposely appear the way you remember them. And they usually exhibit the same personality traits that they had when they were in a physical body so people can identify them. Even though they continue to evolve and grow on the other side, they know how to reveal themselves in a way that their loved ones in our world are able to recognize them. Occasionally, however, souls will show the evolved version of themselves. So be open to that version when you connect with your loved ones.

Most of these souls will share information with you telepathically; they'll send you thoughts, feelings, or visual images. You may see these people with your inner eye. A vision may show up inside your mind or they may reveal where they are in the room. On a rare occasion you may see a flash of light or a faint image with your physical eyes that reveals where the soul is at that time. Some people may hear an actual voice or see a light. However, it is more common to receive information and visual images telepathically.

Doubters may claim it is just your imagination. I understand how people could be skeptical if they've never directly experienced this phenomenon themselves. But the details that come through are usually so specific and so accurate that the odds of it being a result of guessing or using your imagination are way beyond chance.

If you are going to develop your ability to communicate with those on the other side, it's important to believe this is possible and that you are just as capable of communicating with souls on the other side as you are with souls on this side of the veil.

The main reason people have difficulty connecting with those on the other side is because they don't believe they can do it. They believe others may be able to do it but they can't. If I, and many others, can connect with souls on the other side that means *all* of us have that ability. It is a natural ability. Hopefully, the exercise in this chapter will help you develop this ability with confidence.

People may also struggle to make contact with someone who has crossed over because they are emotionally traumatized by their loved one's passing. If you are emotionally distraught, it can be difficult to quiet your mind and get out of your own way so that you can hear or feel your loved ones trying to connect with you. It may be best to wait until you are not so upset by the situation or find someone trustworthy who can make contact for you. It's understandable that you miss your loved one, so be compassionate and patient with yourself.

Your loved one may make contact with you first through your dreams. If you don't sense anyone around or if you don't see him or her in your dreams right away, don't fear that the person just moved on and you'll never again have contact. Sometimes it just takes a while. If you panic or try to force it to happen, you could be disappointed. Breathe and trust that this person will somehow find a way to make contact someday. Just trust that they do see you, they hear you, and they know how you are.

Some people believe they want to connect with their loved ones who have crossed, but subconsciously they are afraid of doing it and so they prevent the experience. They may fear seeing or experiencing something that disturbs them. Or they fear it would be emotionally difficult to reconnect with those they can no longer touch or hold.

And there are many who block this natural ability because they are concerned they could become overwhelmed by their emotions. Or they fear they are too sensitive and will hear the cries from too many souls on the other side. They worry that once they access this ability they won't be able to turn it off. This is the old *victim* consciousness at work again. Carrying this type of fear can limit you. Truthfully, you are a powerful being. You have control over this skill. You can turn it on and off at any time.

If you are afraid to develop this ability, that's okay. You don't need to develop all of the skills that I have mentioned in this book. Even if you don't develop this particular ability, you are still loved and valued—and there are many other ways to expand your consciousness. Just continue to pay attention. This ability could naturally emerge without you working at it intentionally.

Learning to be still and developing a quiet mind usually are helpful when you first begin this process. Subtle information can get lost in an overactive and busy mind. Many people have experienced hearing from departed loved ones in crowded, noisy places, however, so obviously there are no actual rules.

Every person is different. Some people are better at receiving messages while sitting in meditation. Some people recognize signs all around them and know that these signs come from a loved one. For example, one man finds nickels everywhere and knows they are signs from his father. One woman can sense her mother around every time she sees a hummingbird, which was her mother's favorite bird. Of course, these can seem like coincidences to many people—after all, there are hummingbirds in many places. The key was that when she saw it, the woman knew it was her mother sending her a sign.

You can ask for signs or proof that someone is communicating with you. Sometimes souls will find a way to give you that proof. You may hear a meaningful song suddenly play on the radio or see certain numbers pop up on a digital clock. Just be open to signs. And if you listen to your intuition, you'll sense what the message is when you see your sign. Trust the message that arises in your consciousness.

Since most of the time your loved ones will send you telepathic messages, one of the ways to tell if it's a particular person talking to you from the other side is to notice the words and language used. Souls on the other side typically express themselves just as they did on this side so that their loved ones can recognize them. In other words, in your telepathic communication if you hear them use a word that you rarely use, but which he or she always did in life, most likely it is your loved one speaking and not your imagination playing tricks on you.

One highly intelligent soul used exceptionally complicated words that I couldn't even pronounce, let alone understand. I later found out that it was exactly how that person expressed herself in life. I've had others use four-letter words, which I don't use, and then discovered from their family members that the salty language was exactly how that person spoke.

When you are connecting with your loved one, listen carefully and notice how you feel as you hear certain words in your head. Does it sound like your loved one? If it does, then trust you've connected. Be still, ask them questions, listen for answers, and learn to trust whatever you hear. Many people also report feeling physical sensations, such as goose bumps or tingling whenever they connect with loved ones. Trust however this process of communication works for you.

When I first began accessing these intuitive abilities and sharing what I was hearing with other people, I was concerned that what I was sensing was just my imagination. I was so afraid of being wrong that I would limit what I was sharing with people. Over time, I learned that those images and thoughts were almost always right, so I learned to trust and say whatever I heard. The toughest part of sharing information with others is saying the first few words. Once you say the first words, however, then the rest seems to roll out easily. You'll get into a flow and the information will keep coming.

Let me also quickly add that even though I personally have never had any negative experiences in the decades I've been connecting with souls, if you believe you have had a frightening experience with beings on the other side, remember that you have control over any situation. Some people have fearful beliefs, which is what can create fearful experiences. If you have any experience you don't like, you have the power to simply change it or stop the process all together. Just gather your strength and courage, and then tell a soul to go away and not bother you. It's that simple.

If you need more, you can also use other techniques, such as surrounding yourself with white light or asking your guides to surround and protect you. You can also request that your guides remove that soul from your presence. You always have more power than any soul who is on the other side. Don't let society or any scary movie convince you that you are a helpless victim.

There will be those who disagree, who swear that they have been victimized by souls on the other side, and continue to have frightening experiences that they can't control. Moviemakers have done a disservice by teaching this fearful version of those on the other side. Again, I do not want to challenge anyone's beliefs. I continue to believe that our thoughts and beliefs create our reality, however. You are more powerful than *any* experience occurring in your life. Fear can stop you from evolving and developing your true nature. If you do have fear, surround yourself with white light and ask for the highest, most loving experience. That can improve any situation.

ALSO, PAY ATTENTION TO YOUR PETS AND YOUNG CHILDREN. They seem to be very adept at sensing souls on the other side. There are frequent stories of children and animals staring at an empty corner of the room. Watch them for clues that your unseen loved ones are in the room. There are even examples of young children having conversations with relatives on the other side, some whom they've never met in physical form. Life in all its forms, whether seen or unseen, is so much more expansive and amazing than many realize. If you're open to these other experiences, your life can evolve into a whole new adventure.

EXERCISE

This is a guided exercise to help you get started. You can always develop a custom-made exercise that works for you. You don't need to be perfect with this process. Just be open, willing, and do your best. You're safe. You're supported. Many, many people have been able to speak to souls on the other side, so it's obvious that it is a natural skill.

The ability to connect with those on the other side is similar to our ability to imagine, so many people think what they see or hear during this process is just their imagination. For now, trust whatever comes to you. If you stay open and allow someone to show up, if you don't try to force a particular outcome, it will be easier to know that you didn't make the whole thing up. You can ask a particular person to show up, but it may serve you more in the beginning just to see who arrives spontaneously.

What you see with your inner eye is often much more trustworthy than what you see with your physical eyes. The physical senses deceive us all the time. So learn to trust what your internal vision is showing you.

Step 1. Relax.
Find a comfortable location where you won't be disturbed, take deep breaths until you feel peaceful and relaxed. You are safe and supported. Take your time when you do this process. Remain patient, calm, and relaxed.

Step 2. Trust.
For now put aside any doubts you've had about this being possible, and allow visions and thoughts to come to you. Just relax and allow it to be easy.

As you slowly breathe in, imagine your whole body being filled with white light. See that light also surround you. Then, see the light expand and fill your entire environment. White light is everywhere. It's a beautiful and calming white light. You feel peaceful.

Take more deep breaths and feel yourself relax even more deeply into this wonderful essence.

Imagine that a loving being gently steps out of the white light. This is one of your spiritual guides here to assist you with this exercise. Your guides are always around you. Notice what this particular being looks like and how you feel.

There is immense love radiating from this being. You are safe and supported. Those on the other side are delighted that you are willing to talk with them.

This guiding being has something important to say to you. So take a moment and listen to the message. Hearing this being is easy. It's a very helpful message so be still and just listen now. This message is filled with love, so you can trust that it's for your benefit.

Feeling relaxed and comfortable, you can now ask this guide anything. So quietly ask your guide any questions you have. Then be still and listen for the answers. Take a moment now to do this.

This being surrounds you and fills you with unconditional love. You now see that everything has always been fine—you have always been loved and supported. Even when you went through challenging times, you had help and guidance all around you.

Now, with this guide still there, supporting you and helping you, see another being quietly emerge from the light. It's someone that you know. Notice the appearance. This being is smiling and radiating love toward you. This soul is very happy living on the other side.

This being has been around you for a while . . . and also has an important message for you. This message will help you. It's easy to hear this soul. Quiet your mind and listen.

You can ask either of these beings questions now. What would you like to know? Take a moment now and ask your questions.

These beings are sending you loving energy right now. Notice where all the energy goes. Is it healing something in your body or is it being sent to your heart? Where are they sending all that loving energy? Breathe and take it in. You are safe to open up and accept it.

Ask them now if they have any guidance that can help you live a happy and healthy life. What do you need to know to live that wonderful life? Listen. Is there anything you need to do?

These souls are sending you pure love. Notice if there is anything else they want to say to you. Listen carefully to their words.

With all the light surrounding you, you can sense now how many loving souls are in that light. We are all connected with it. These beings are always in your world and you can call on them any time.

Step 3. Return to alert.
Take a deep breath and return to a fully aware state of consciousness. Take another deep cleansing breath and feel your entire body fill with strong life energy. Slowly move your body around. Be aware of every part of your body: your back, legs, arms, stomach, neck, and everything else. Feel your healthy and vibrant body.

Remember you are always loved and safe. The universe is filled with love and light.

THE BENEFITS OF COMMUNICATING
WITH THE OTHER SIDE

The ability to communicate with loved ones who have left their *physical* bodies can be very comforting to friends and family. It can reduce suffering and sorrow. It can create healing for those left behind. And it reinforces that we always have a continuous connection.

This ability broadens our perception of who we are. It removes the mental blinders that separate us from the unseen universe. It can also reduce our fear of death. Knowing that we continue can affect the way we live our lives. It can help us become more adventurous and go after our dreams rather than always playing it safe.

Also, imagine what we could learn about humanity, life, and the nature of reality from those on the other side, those with a less restrictive perspective than ours. I have learned many astounding things by connecting with people who have crossed over. I've learned that we are eternal beings, and that time doesn't exist—so all our lives are happening simultaneously.

Souls on the other side tell us that we are loved unconditionally no matter what, that we are being taken care of, that we are not alone, and that our loved ones are still around us. These souls also verify that there is no punishment after life. As soon as we cross over, we realize the reasons behind our behavior here. And we experience the effects that our words and actions had on us and on others. These souls share that we have free will, that our old concept of an anthropomorphic God is very limited, and that God or the Om is much more expansive, powerful, and loving than we know. Imagine what more we could learn from these souls.

Those who have had near-death experiences and those who communicate with us from the other side share similar insights. They report that our brains act like filters and actually block grand truths and experiences from us. Our brains tell us we are separate from everything and limits our ability to see our true expansiveness. Supposedly, at least until now, having limited awareness is what has been necessary for us to have a physical experience here. The brain defines our individual identities so we can experience being separate from everything else; but it also limits our understanding of the greater "I am." Many of us are now ready to have grander and more aware experiences in life.

Knowing this information and having transcendent experiences can bring us to a whole new level of understanding of life, reality, and our true abilities. We don't have to function from the old, limited paradigm any more. We are evolving and gaining insight into our true nature. You can still experience a physical world, you'll just have more freedom and power to create better experiences with this expanded awareness and these enhanced abilities.

THEIR INFORMATION

Souls on the other side share that people have different experiences at the moment of their crossing. What people experience appears to be tied to their beliefs. Some people meet angels, saints, or Christ. Others meet Buddha, Mohammed, or other beloved spiritual teachers. Loved ones who have departed before are always there to greet us with unconditional love.

Those who have no belief in the afterlife are often surprised when they cross over to see that not only do they still exist, but that life feels more real on that side, as if this side of the veil is the dream and the other side is reality. They often report seeing vibrant colors that we don't see here, and hearing sounds that we don't perceive in our physical realm. Everyone is treated with unconditional love, respect, and patience on the other side.

Only a few of the souls I've communicated with say that they temporarily experienced a deep quiet or a fearful situation when they first crossed over, but that only lasted until they were rescued. Those situations appear to have been created by their beliefs about themselves or death. No one was allowed to stay stuck in any belief-driven illusion for too long. Eventually a guide came to bring them to the experience of unconditional love and peace. In these cases, I'm sure the prayers and loving thoughts of loved ones helped those people move more quickly beyond their fear-based illusions. If souls need to work with guides for a while, they receive extra help. I've heard from more than one transitioned person that they were "slow learners." Guides and teachers helped them understand their life experiences here and why they acted in life the way that they did.

Some people experience a powerful, all-loving light and a life review immediately. They simultaneously see and feel everything they ever experienced in this life. They also feel every emotion they ever caused another person to feel. They feel the same joy or hurt that their words or actions caused another to feel. Then they feel what that person's actions caused the next person to feel, and so on. They discover that their actions had created a ripple effect, and they feel the feelings of every person who was ever affected. They describe it as becoming everyone who was ever touched by them, no matter how far the ripple went from its origin with them.

Some report having full knowledge of every lifetime they have ever had, but also share that all of those lifetimes are all still occurring now, not in the past.

Eventually, everyone reaches a state of bliss and unconditional love. Some of the souls I've spoken with have reported becoming suddenly aware that we are all connected. Everything is one consciousness, one mind, and one being.

What these souls have shared from the other side is that they, like we, have free will. They are free to create anything they desire, they can have any experience they choose, and they can travel anywhere they want just by imagining it. They retain a sense of self, albeit a more expansive sense of self. And they do continue to exist.

One young man who had crossed unexpectedly was temporarily choosing to hang out at his favorite surf spot in Mexico with his dog, which had also recently crossed over. This was his "heaven," the spot that brought him the most joy. The man reported he could stay there for as long as he wanted. Departed souls have free will. Eventually, souls choose to move on to other experiences. We continue to be curious and adventurous beings.

Personally, I have never experienced a soul on the other side who was suffering or in despair. Souls continue to spend time near their embodied loved ones because they want to do so, not because they have unfinished business or an unhealthy attachment to the physical realm. Occasionally, I have heard from deceased loved ones that they were around beloved family members here because they were trying to help those living members resolve regret, anger, or hurt. The living relative may need to hear an apology from the departed, and the departed is always willing to oblige. They have better insight on the other side and have no need or desire to carry a grudge.

I know other people have had different experiences than I have and feel the need to help a departed soul *go to the light.* I honor people's different beliefs and experiences. I'm just sharing that this has not been my experience with any soul who has crossed over. They are already connected with the light. Actually we all are. It's just that we've forgotten. Once souls transition to the other side, most remember who they really are. They realize what their lives were about, they know they are always connected with loved ones, and they know they can choose to remain nearby or move on to other experiences. Actually, we're always connected no matter how far apart we may seem to travel from one another.

There seems to be many different levels of consciousness and experiences. Some of these souls report they will be experiencing other lives here again. Call it reincarnation or other lives, whichever you'd like. Others remain on that side for some time, conversing with loved ones or meeting with elevated teachers and thinkers on that side. Others who have crossed over often act as guides for people on this side. I've heard multiple times that someone on that side has chosen to be a guide for people who are struggling here, or that they are now guiding different healers, teachers, world leaders, artists, children, family members, and so forth on this side. They can choose to be helpers from that side of the veil, just as we can choose to be helpers on this side.

They also report that they are free to move on to other levels of consciousness, other realms of existence, to have other experiences. It's challenging for us to understand certain concepts with our limited version of time and space. In the physical realm, we typically think in linear terms. We grow wiser over time or we move up the ladder in our jobs, so we assume there are similar progressions on the other side.

But actually, as souls we have experiences that cause us to evolve in all directions, so it's best not to think in terms of one straight line of progress. We are not one-directional, linear beings. We are ever-expanding, always experiencing, infinite beings. We are infinite expressions of All That Is or Universal Intelligence, which is always creating and experiencing. In other words, as we have any experience in any lifetime or any realm, we become more: We add to our consciousness and the consciousness of all.

Despite our tendency to think in linear terms and despite what we've been taught, spiritual evolution doesn't mean that we reach higher and higher levels of consciousness as if there are hierarchies, or that the goal is to move closer to some ultimate, supreme level of consciousness because that presupposes then an ultimate, finite top level. At some point then we must reach the pinnacle and have nowhere else to go, nothing else to experience.

We can become more aware or happier in the different realms, but in reality we will never be anything less than majestic and divine creators. We often believe that angels or spiritual guides are better or more evolved than we are. But all souls are magnificent beings. None is greater than or less than any other. Beings are just having different experiences, doing different jobs, and currently may have a clearer perspective than we do because they are not living in this mesmerizing physical realm. But we are all equally treasured, unconditionally loved, and valued. We are all perfect expressions and manifestations of God or Source.

An interesting phenomenon that some people find challenging to grasp is that we are both in physical incarnations and in between lives simultaneously. Your real identity is as an oversoul, a greater soul that remains fully intact and fully aware while various aspects of you adventure into different lifetimes and different realms. Think of an octopus with eight arms that extend out in different directions, each touching different things and having different experiences. We can use that analogy to describe your oversoul and the many different expressions of you that are going into diverse lifetimes to have a multitude of unique experiences. And you exist beyond time and space, so it's not even accurate to say the greater you is limited to living in a different realm. You are beyond realms.

WHAT THE ABILITY TO SPEAK TO THE OTHER SIDE REVEALS

Being able to speak to people who no longer have physical bodies proves that our consciousness exists beyond our brains and bodies, and that we are unbounded in time and space. It proves that we are not mere biological machines that age, then die and cease to exist. There is more to our existence than biology.

Being guided by the two young men in the Mohave Desert who had already crossed over to the location where their bodies were proved to me once again that we have exceptional abilities and that we are more remarkable than we've been taught. If we are able to speak to people on the other side, to those who are no longer in physical bodies, what else is possible that we don't know about yet?

The possibility of talking to souls on the other side expands our concept of ourselves and reality. Life is much bigger than we imagined because it extends far beyond the limited version of the world we've been taught to detect with our five physical senses.

THE SCIENCE

Many physicians believe that people who have near-death experiences are just experiencing the effects of the brain shutting down, and assert that what these people have seen can be explained by neurobiology. But there are cases, such as that of neurosurgeon Eben Alexander, M.D., author of *Proof of Heaven,* whose neocortex, the part of the brain that is responsible for memory, sensory perception, spatial reasoning, motor commands, conscious language, thought processes and every part of experience in consciousness, was so damaged that it wasn't functioning at all. Therefore, Dr. Alexander knew for himself that his brain couldn't have been hallucinating or creating the "hyper real" experiences he had during his NDE.[1] Also, doctors are at a loss to explain how he miraculously survived his usually fatal condition.

And as we have seen, I also can communicate with people who no longer have functioning brains; they are dead. I do not just pick up information psychically from their living loved ones, because many times those people do not actually know the details that are shared. Only the people who have crossed over know the information and are able to share it; and eventually those left behind are able to confirm its veracity. The two boys in the ravine is a case in point.

There is growing interest in researching consciousness. Many physicists are now questioning our old, narrow, materialistic definition of reality. There are too many people having unusual experiences and witnessing phenomenon that cannot be explained by classical physics. Many of us reveal that consciousness is not limited to the brain.

For more information and a list of some of the physicists who are researching consciousness and near-death experiences, see the Resources section at the back of the book.

SPIRITUALITY

Different spiritual cultures disagree over theology and dogma. Each has a different explanation for our genesis, the purpose of our existence, which groups God favors, what happens to the soul after death, and more. Most spiritual traditions do agree, however, that the soul continues living after death. Some of them also teach that our soul exists before our current physical incarnation. But none of them share the exact same version of what happens after death. Souls on the other side explaining that they have free will and that their experiences when they first cross over are influenced by their beliefs, could account for the variation in the different spiritual teachings.

While strict classical physics does not support the concept of an afterlife, quantum physics seems to be the bridge that is bringing science and spirituality together.

The afterlife seems to hold great mystery, although more and more people are having contact with souls on the other side so secrets are being revealed. The veil between the worlds seems to be getting thinner.

CHAPTER NINE

EXPLORING FURTHER

"Any sufficiently advanced technology is indistinguishable
from magic."
—ARTHUR C. CLARKE

W hat does technology have to do with our evolution in
consciousness?

TECHNOLOGY AND EVOLUTION

We take for granted the mindboggling technologies that can
broadcast invisible signals from a television station's tower to a
satellite located thousands of miles above Earth and then send
those signals back down to individual television sets. Then,
somehow, those signals turn into a myriad of little lights blinking
on and off on our screen, and makes it appear as if real people are
moving around on the screen.

We also nonchalantly accept that our voices can turn into tiny
bits of information that travel from our cell phones across miles
and miles of space, and somehow find their way specifically and

exactly to a friend's phone on the other side of the world. And then those tiny bits of information are converted once again into sounds and words that we can understand. How in the world does this happen? And why don't those bits of information collide or interfere with other bits of information as they travel through the air?

We accept that smartphones, satellites, and the Internet can almost instantaneously send and receive signals all over the world. But we haven't yet fully accepted that our minds (not synonymous with "brains") have the same capability. We think it's only technology that is capable of these incredible feats.

We may be creating these different technologies to show us, or remind us, of what we are capable of doing ourselves. Technology may be revealing that we are actually capable of doing the same things *without* technology. Consciousness uses the same principles as technology. Or is it that technology is reflecting or revealing consciousness?

Technology seems to be further connecting us. Even though many complain that people have become less social, because we are texting rather than talking to one another, technology has also made us much more aware of people around the world. There is a global *web* that now connects us and is helping us learn more about each other. It's made us more compassionate toward others around the world because we now know more about their plights. This technology may actually lead to the development of our telepathic abilities by furthering our connection.

While we trust that the technology experts can create, demonstrate, and explain to us how our gadgets work (and most of these advanced gadgets exist because of quantum physics), there are also many other *experts* who are revealing what amazing natural abilities humans have.

WHAT CAN STOP US?

Holding fast to our old beliefs about reality and who we are can prevent us from reaching our ultimate potential and achieving what is possible. We have taught ourselves limited concepts about life and fed our egos, our self-identities, false information. Fortunately, there have always been adventurous explorers and risk takers willing to push the boundaries who have moved us beyond our old limitations. Maybe you are one of those people, too.

It's only fear, our egos, our limiting beliefs, and our stories that can stop us.

THE EGO

Many people judge the ego. However, if we criticize our ego or label any part of us "bad," we could hold back on using our authentic power and developing our full capabilities. If we don't trust ourselves since we identify with our egos, or fear that we could make a mistake and cause harm to another, we could stop our progress.

The ego is not the fullness of who we really are. The ego can't see beyond what we've taught it to believe. Our higher selves therefore need to be in charge of our lives, not our egos.

We need to educate the ego and help it evolve. We need to see the ego for what it is: an aspect of us that was created to perceive and interact with the physical world, just like the eye was created to help us perceive and navigate the physical world. We've trained the ego to think small by giving it false information. Of course, neither the eye nor the ego is bad. Both just have *limited perception*. If we relied on our eyes to give us a complete version of reality, we would be in trouble. Your eyes don't see the fire truck that your ears can hear coming up behind you, nor do they smell the smoke from a nearby fire. The eyes, like the ego, have limited perception.

Be loving and patient with your ego. You have fed it limited, often fear-based information and that's what it believes now. You've given it an inadequate and faulty description of you. You've insisted that you have limitations and you've defined reality very narrowly. When you try to stretch outside those strict boundaries, your ego gets frightened and stops you in an attempt to keep you safe. Your ego tries to protect you and help you logically navigate life, but it only feels safe with certain things.

To change your life and move beyond your ego's fears, you don't need to judge your ego, but to feed it better, more empowering information. Think of it like a child. If you tell a child that the world is a scary place, that terrible things could harm her if she left the security of her safe little home, and then you get angry with that child for screaming and throwing a tantrum when you try to get her into the car to go somewhere, can you see how you might be the one responsible for the situation, not the child?

Rather than push that frightened and resistant child into the car, wouldn't it make more sense to teach her different, more empowering things about herself and the world? That's what we have been doing in this book: educating the ego, giving it more expansive information about reality.

CHANGING OUR BELIEFS CAN BE CHALLENGING, especially if we've been holding limited perceptions of life and ourselves for a long time. When we believe something, we gather evidence to support those beliefs. Over the years, we have built quite a strong foundation to uphold and fortify those limiting beliefs. We have convinced ourselves that what we see in the world and what we experience is the truth about reality, not just our *beliefs* about reality. Hopefully, the new information you've learned will assist you in shifting some of your limiting beliefs. Together, all of us have created a very convincing version of reality—but it may not be the real version.

Live with whatever beliefs make you comfortable and choose how you want to live. You have free will. We all have different beliefs, perspectives, and life experiences. But when you find yourself feeling stuck, fearful, or unhappy don't blame your ego. Comfort and educate your ego, challenge your beliefs by recognizing they are just beliefs about reality, not reality itself. Practice thinking more expansive thoughts. Also look for beliefs that are more empowering, loving, and life affirming, even if those new beliefs don't feel quite real yet.

Continue to focus on your new desirable beliefs and begin gathering evidence to support those new beliefs. Then your ego can better assist you and will create fewer fear-based obstacles for you. Your ego is here to serve you. It's a part of you, and you're in this together.

OUR STORIES

The other thing that can hold us back is our attachment to our stories. We spend so much of our time and energy on our personal stories that there is very little time left to explore outside of our "box." We can even hold on to the story that we are not capable of accessing the abilities of our infinite selves, or that these abilities are not real.

We're creators who love to create. We're such splendid writers, directors, producers, and actors that our stories can be very convincing. They feel real. We often create stories based on our limited beliefs about reality though. And out of habit, we can spend most of our time and energy focused on the same repetitive stories, struggles, and dramas, or on stories that distract us. Unfortunately, our egos can become addicted to these stories and the emotions they generate. We easily forget that they're just stories. We think that's the way life is. Your attachment to your stories can keep you stuck in an old world.

We forget that we can change our stories, that we can just turn the page and create again. You are a more powerful creator than you know. So learn how to create stories that you enjoy. Hopefully realizing that you have greater powers and abilities will help you create more life-enhancing stories.

CONCLUSION

"Ye are gods."
—*THE BIBLE,* JOHN 10:34

W hat I've shared are just some of our inherent abilities. Many more are possible. Quantum physics allows for the ability to travel back in time, walk through walls, walk on water, turn water to wine, not age or die, and more. You probably haven't explored all these abilities in this universe yet, but you're probably enjoying many of them in parallel universes.

Many people appear to be accepting these ideas now, meaning that living with these abilities will eventually be commonplace in our culture. But just as it took a while for people to accept that the world was round and even longer for them to take full advantage of its roundness, it may take a little while for all of us to activate our natural capabilities. It's important to start somewhere. Every person who develops these skills will add to the emerging consciousness.

HEAVEN ON EARTH

There are many people today suffering hardships; some even admit they look forward to the day they are free from the confines of this physical world. They yearn for heaven or nirvana. They want to experience more ease, peace, and spiritual connection, and they believe those experiences exist somewhere else and at some future time. This yearning arises because they've forgotten who they really are and what they are capable of creating right here, right now.

You don't have to die and go to heaven or nirvana to experience bliss or a stronger spiritual connection. We're collectively starting to create *heaven* on Earth right here. We're in the process of awakening to it. We can once again live in the garden that this realm was created to be. We can play as happy creators. If you are someone who believes that this plane of existence is meant to be a school, remember: Even schools have playgrounds. Learning and evolving can be fun.

You have the natural power to create magnificent love, joy, peace, prosperity, and radiant health in your life right here, right now. If you could grasp who you authentically are and activate your true abilities, you would experience so much more and you could add so much more beauty and love to the world. We're all connected and we're all changing.

This may be why you came to this realm at this time. You may be part of the team that is here to bring an advanced level of awareness and higher quality life experiences to the planet so we can have more freedom, love, and joy right here, right now. You live in an aware, loving, and infinite universe (multiverse). We're not passive beings who are meant to sit meditatively in a cave our whole lives. We are creators who are meant to create. May you be courageous enough to jump up off the paper and live your greatest potential. And may we all once again remember how to fully enjoy our life adventures!

ACKNOWLEDGEMENTS

My heartfelt appreciation goes out to everyone in my life. I am grateful for your love and light. And to you who supported the creation of this book, and helped bring the book to life, thank you sincerely for your support, guidance, and patience. It is fun to create and play with all of you.

Resources

Resources

Visit Pamala's Website

www.LifeColorsCity.com
Discover your aura colors, read Pamala's blog, listen to her radio show, watch videos, and enjoy other features. You can also become a premium member and discover greater in depth information about you, your relationships, career, health, money, family, and more.

Connect with Pamala on the Social Networks

Facebook: https://www.facebook.com/PamOslie
Facebook: https://www.facebook.com/auracolors
Facebook: https://www.facebook.com/LoveColorsAura
Twitter: https://twitter.com/LoveColorsAura
Google+: https://plus.google.com/+Lifecolorscity/posts

Read Pamala's Books

Life Colors: What the Colors in Your Aura Reveal.
   New World Library, 2000.
*Make Your Dreams Come True: Simple Steps for Changing the
   Beliefs That Limit You.* Amber-Allen Publishing, 1998.
Love Colors: A New Approach to Love, Relationships, and Auras.
   New World Library, 2007.

RECOMMENDED READING

To become as knowledgeable as I can about a subject, I study, ask questions, and experiment with the information to see if it's true for me. I study some of the most cutting-edge thinkers to see what they know—especially to see if they can explain why I can do what I can do. I not only fervently study quantum physics and spiritual teachings, but I also do my best to apply new information to my life. I tend to push the boundaries.

There are many things we don't know yet about our capabilities and the nature of the multiverse. In case you're interested in learning more, I put together a list of recommended books, articles, and videos by some of the sages and scientists who have published important research in their fields. These are included below.

Pamala's Favorite Books

If you decide you want to make a quantum leap in your understanding of the sorts of ideas presented in *Infinite You,* my favorite books are those in the Seth series by Jane Roberts. I believe those books were ahead of their time. They transformed my life and are responsible for the activation of my expanded abilities.

Richard Bach. Illusions: *The Adventures of a Reluctant Messiah.* Arrow Books, 2001 (originally published 1978).

Richard Bach. *Jonathan Livingston Seagull.* Scribner, 2006 (originally published 1970).

Deepak Chopra. *Creating Affluence: The A-to-Z Steps to a Richer Life.* New World Library/Amber-Allen Publishing, 1998.

Deepak Chopra. *The Seven Spiritual Laws of Success: A Practical Guide to the Fulfillment of Your Dreams.* New World Library/Amber-Allen Publishing, 1994.

Jane Roberts. *Dreams, "Evolution," and Value Fulfillment, Volume 1: A Seth Book.* Amber-Allen Publishing, 1997 (originally published 1986).

Jane Roberts. *Dreams, "Evolution," and Value Fulfillment, Volume 2: A Seth Book.* Amber-Allen Publishing, 1997 (originally published 1986).

Jane Roberts. *The Individual and the Nature of Mass Events: A Seth Book.* Amber-Allen Publishing, 1995.

Jane Roberts. *The Magical Approach: Seth Speaks About the Art of Creative Living.* Amber-Allen Publishing, 1995.

Jane Roberts. *The Nature of Personal Reality: Specific, Practical Techniques for Solving Everyday Problems and Enriching the Life You Know.* Amber-Allen Publishing/New World Library, 1994 (originally published 1974).

Jane Roberts. *The Nature of the Psyche: Its Human Expression.* Amber-Allen Publishing, 1996.

Jane Roberts. *The Seth Material: The Spiritual Teacher that Launched the New Age.* New Awareness Network, 2010 (originally published 1970).

Jane Roberts. *Seth Speaks: The Eternal Validity of the Soul.* Amber-Allen Publishing, 1994 (originally published 1972).

Jane Roberts. *The "Unknown" Reality, Volume 1: A Seth Book.* Amber-Allen Publishing, 1996 (originally published 1977).

Jane Roberts. *The "Unknown" Reality, Volume 2: A Seth Book.* Amber-Allen Publishing, (originally published 1979).

Jane Roberts. *The Way Toward Health: A Seth Book.* Amber-Allen Publishing, 1997.

On Consciousness and Energy

Georges Dupenois, "Mind, Matter, and Reality," *The Philosopher,* vol. 88, no. 1. Philosophical Society of England website: http://www.the-philosopher.co.uk/mind&mat.htm.

Amit Goswami. *The Self-Aware Universe: How Consciousness Creates the Material World.* J.P. Tarcher/Putnam, 1993.

Journal of Consciousness Studies. Imprint Academic (United Kingdom) website: http://www.imprint.co.uk/jcs.html.

Robert Lanza. *Biocentrism: How Life and Consciousness Are the Keys to Understanding the True Nature of the Universe.* BenBella Books, 2010.

Leonard Susskind. *The Cosmic Landscape: String Theory and the Illusion of Intelligent Design.* Little, Brown and Company, 2005.

Michael Talbot. *Beyond the Quantum.* Scribner, 1987.

William A. Tiller, Walter E. Dibble, Jr., and Michael J. Kohane. *Conscious Acts of Creation.* Pavior Publishing, 2001.

On the Holographic Principle

Niels Bohr. *Essays 1932–1957 on Atomic Physics and Human Knowledge: The Philosophical Writings of Niels Bohr, Volume 2.* Ox Bow Press, 1987.

Niels Bohr. *Atomic Theory and the Description of Nature: 1.* Ox Bow Press, 1987.

Raphael Bousso, "The Holographic Principle," *Reviews of Modern Physics* vol. 74, no. 3 (August 2002): p. 825.

Richard P. Feynman, Robert Leighton, and Matthew Sands. *The Feynman Lectures on Physics, Volume 3: Quantum Mechanics.* Addison-Wesley, 1965.

Leonard Susskind, "The World as a Hologram," *Journal of Mathematical Physics,* vol. 36, no. 11 (September 1995): pp. 6377–96.

Michael Talbot. *The Holographic Universe: The Revolutionary Theory of Reality.* HarperCollins Publishers, 1991.

On Intuition, Telepathy, and Psychic Abilities

Dean Radin. *Entangled Minds: Extrasensory Experiences in a Quantum Reality.* Paraview Pocket Books, 2006.

On Energy Fields and Auras

Barbara Bowers. *What Color is Your Aura? Personality Spectrums for Understanding and Growth.* Pocket Books, 1989.

David G. Boyers and William A. Tiller, "Corona Discharge Photography," *Journal of Applied Physics,* vol. 44, no. 7 (1973): pp. 3102–12.

Seymon Kirlian, and Valentina Kirlian, "Photography and Visual Observation by Means of High-Frequency Currents," *Journal of Scientific and Applied Photography*, vol. 6, no. 6 (1963).

Konstantin Korotkov. *Energy Fields Electrophotonic Analysis in Humans and Nature*. EBookIt.com, 2012.

Manjir Samanta-Laughton, "Quantum Bio-cosmology: The Science of Auras and Chakras," *Holistic Health*, no. 79 (Winter 2003/2004).

John Opalinski, "Kirlian-type Images and the Transport of Thin-film Materials in High-voltage Corona Discharges," *Journal of Applied Physics*, vol. 50, no. 1 (1979): pp. 498–504.

Beverly Rubik. *The Interrelationship Between Mind and Matter.* Center for Frontier Sciences/Temple University, 1992.

Beverly Rubik. *Life at the Edge of Science: An Anthology of Papers by Beverly Rubik.* Institute for Frontier Science, 1996.

Gary Schwartz with William L. Simon. *The Energy Healing Experiments: Science Reveals Our Natural Power to Heal.* Atria Books, 2007.

William A. Tiller. *Science and Human Transformation: Subtle Energies, Intentionality and Consciousness.* Pavior Publishing, 1997.

On Parallel Universes

Peter Byrne. *The Many Worlds of Hugh Everett III: Multiple Universes, Mutual Assured Destruction, and the Meltdown of a Nuclear Family.* Oxford University Press, 2010.

David Deutsch. *The Beginning of Infinity: Explanations That Transform the World.* Penguin Books, 2001.

David Deutsch. *The Fabric of Reality: The Science of Parallel Universes—and Its Implications.* Penguin Books, 1998.

David Deutsch. "The Structure of the Multiverse," Cornell University Library (April 2001). Website: www.arxiv.org/abs/quant-ph/0104033.

Hugh Everett, III, "The Theory of the Universal Wave Function," in B.S. Dewitt and R.N. Graham (editors), *The Many-Worlds Interpretation of University of Quantum Mechanics: Princeton Series in Physics.* Princeton University Press, 1973.

Michael Clive Price, "FAQ on the Everett Interpretation." Website: www.physics.wustl.edu/alford/many_worlds_FAQ.html.

Rebecca Sato, "New Proof from Oxford: Parallel Universes Exist," *Daily Galaxy* (posted September 25, 2007). Website: www.dailygalaxy.com/my_weblog/2007/09/n--one-of-the-m.html.

David Wallace. *The Emergent Multiverse: Quantum Theory According to the Everett Interpretation.* Oxford University Press, 2012.

David Wallace, "The Everett Interpretation," in R. Batterman (editor), *The Oxford Handbook of Philosophy of Physics.* Oxford University Press, 2013.

David Wallace, "A Prolegomenon to the Ontology of the Everett Interpretation," in A. Ney and D. Albert (editors), *The Wave Function: Essays in the Metaphysics of Quantum Mechanics.* Oxford University Press, 2013.

On Other (Past) Lives

Jenny Cockell. *Yesterday's Children: The Search for My Family from the Past.* Piatkus Books, 1993.

Jim Tucker. *Life Before Life: Children's Memories of Previous Lives.* St. Martin's Press, 2005.

Brian Weiss. *Many Lives, Many Masters: The True Story of a Prominent Psychiatrist, His Young Patient, and the Past-Life Therapy That Changed Both Their Lives*. Fireside, 1988.

Brian Weiss and Amy: *Miracles Happen: The Transformational Healing Power of Past Life Memories*. Harper One, 2012.

Michael Talbot. *Your Past Lives*. Fawcett Books, 1989.

On Physics and Philosophy

Fred Alan Wolf. *Dr. Quantum's Little Book of Big Ideas: Where Science Meets Spirit*. Moment Point Press, 2008.

Fred Alan Wolf. *Time Loops and Space Twists: How God Created the Universe*. Hierophant Publishing,, 2013.

Werner Heisenberg. *Physics and Philosophy: The Revolution in Modern Science*. Harper Perennial Modern Classics, 2007.

Erwin Schrödinger. My View of the World. Ox Bow Press, 1983.

Anton Zeilinger, "Experiment and the Foundations of Quantum Physics," *Review of Modern Physics,* vol. 71 (1999): pp. S288–97.

Recommended Videos

Through the Wormhole (Discovery Channel). Website: http://science.discovery.com/tv-shows/through-the-wormhole.

Think Quest Library. Oracle Education Foundation Website: http://thinkquest.org/pls/html/think.library.

Fred Alan Wolf. "What If All Is an Illusion?" TEDxReset, 2011. Watch on YouTube: http://www.youtube.com/watch?v=Q9d_HYkS9Pc.

PSI RESEARCH FACILITIES, SOCIETIES, ASSOCIATIONS, AND INSTITUTES

The following organizations are doing cutting-edge research on psionic (psi) abilities, such as telepathy, telekinesis, psychokinesis, and extrasensory perception. Some also offer lectures, courses, and workshops.

American Society for Psychical Research
5 West 73rd Street
New York, New York 10023
Phone: 1 (212) 799-5050
Website: http://www.aspr.com

Anomalistic Psychology Research Unit
Goldsmiths, University of London New Cross London SE14 6NW England
Phone: (44) 20-7919-7171
Website: http://www.gold.ac.uk

British Institute of Kirlian Photography
Website: http://kirlianphotography.webs.com/history.htm

Center for Consciousness Studies
P.O. Box 210068
Tucson, AZ. 85721-0068
Website: http://www.consciousness.arizona.edu/
TSC2011Plenary1BrainFields.htm

Cognitive Sciences Laboratory
Phone: 1 (650) 473-0817
Website: http://www.lfr.org/lfr/csl

C. I. R. P. Centro Interdisciplinare Ricerca Parapsicologica
Website: http://xoomer.virgilio.it/mariafel/CIRPENG.html

Division of Perceptual Studies, University of Virginia
P.O. Box 800152
Charlottesville, VA. 22908
Phone: 1 (434) 924-2281
Website: http://www.medicine.virginia.edu/clinical/
departments/
psychiatry/sections/cspp/dops

Exceptional Human Experience Network
EHE Network 414 Rockledge Road New Bern, N.C. 28562
Phone: (919) 636-8734
Website: http://www.ehe.org/display/splash.html

Fondazione Biblioteca Bozzano-De Boni
Via Guglielmo Marconi, 8
40122 Bologna
Italy
Phone: (39) 51-272021-554033
Website:
http://www.bibliotecabozzanodeboni.com/website/english

Global Consciousness Project
Website: http://noosphere.princeton.edu

Institut fuer Grenzgebiete der Psychologie und Psychohygiene
Wilhelmstrasse 3a
D-79098 Freiburg i. Br.
Germany
Phone: (49) 0761-20721-0
Website: http://www.igpp.de/english/welcome.htm

Institut Metapsychique International
51, Rue de l'Aqueduc
75010, Paris
France
Phone: (33) 1-46-07-23-85
Website: http://www.metaphysique.org

Institute of Noetic Sciences
625 Second Street, Suite 200
Petaluma, CA. 94952
Website: http://ions.org
Phone: (707) 781-7420

Institute of Paranormal Psychology
(Instituto de Psicología Paranormal)
Salta 2015
C1137ACQ, Buenos Aires.
Argentina
Phone: (54) 11-4305-6724
Website: http://www.alipsi.com.ar/english.asp

International Association for Near-Death Studies
2741 Campus Walk Avenue, Building 500
Durham, N.C. 27705-8878
Phone: (919) 383-7940
Website: http://iands.org/home.html

International Research Institute
40A, Yuuki Building
Sonno 1108-2
Inage, Chiba 263-0051
Japan
Phone: (81) 43-255-5481
Website: http://www.a-iri.org/iri-jp

International Society of Life Information Science
Yuuki Bldg., 1108-2 Sonno,
Inage, Chiba-shi, 263-0051
Japan
Phone: (81) 43-255-5481
Website: http://www.islis.a-iri.org/en/journalE.htm

International Society for the Study of Subtle Energies and Energy Medicine
11005 Ralston Road, Suite 100D
Arvada, CO. 80004
Phone: 1 (303) 425-4625
Website: http://www.issseem.org

Koestler Parapsychology Unit
Department of Psychology
University of Edinburgh
7 George Square
Edinburgh EH8 9JZ
Scotland
Phone: (44) 131-650-3348
Website: http://www.koestler-parapsychology.psy.ed.ac.uk

Laboratories for Fundamental Research
Phone: 1 (650) 327-2007
Website: http://www.lfr.org

Pacific Neuropsychiatric Institute
Seattle Healing Arts Center 6300 Ninth Ave N.E., Suite 353
Seattle, WA. 98115 Tel: 1 (206) 527-6289
Website: http://www.pni.org

Princeton Engineering Anomalies Research
C-131, Engineering Quadrangle
Princeton University
Princeton, N.J. 08544
Phone: 1 (609) 258-5950
Website: http://www.princeton.edu/~pear

Rhine Research Center/Institute for Parapsychology
2741 Campus Walk Avenue, Building 500
Durham, N.C. 27705
Phone: 1 (919) 688-8241
Website: http://rhine.org

Society for Psychical Research
49 Marloes Road
Kensington, London W8 6LA
England
Phone: (44) 207-937-8984
Website: http://www.spr.ac.uk/main

Notes

Introduction

Epigraph. Albert Einstein. The source of this quote is uncertain. It has been theorized that it comes from a letter to the family of his lifelong friend Michele Besso, after learning of his death (March 1955), which ends: "Now he has departed from this strange world a little ahead of me. That means nothing. People like us, who believe in physics, know that the distinction between past, present, and future is only a stubbornly persistent illusion." As quoted in Freeman Dyson, *Disturbing the Universe* (New York: Basic Books, 1979): p. 193.

1. Scientists conclude that spacetime is the fourth dimension. See Projects by Students for Students, "Time According to Einstein's Theory of Relativity," Oracle ThinkQuest Education Foundation website (accessed November 2013): http://library.thinkquest.org/06aug/02088/einstein.htm.
   Also see: James Overduin, "Einstein's Spacetime," Gravity Probe B website (posted November 2007):
   http://einstein.stanford.edu/SPACETIME/spacetime2.html.

2. Some physicists have theorized that time may go backward and forward—and sideways (into parallel universes). See Ben Goertzel, "On the Physics and Phenomenology of Time," website: http://www.goertzel.org/papers/timepap. html.
   Also see Tim Folger, "Newsflash: Time May Not Exist," Discover (June 12, 2007) website:
   http://discovermagazine.com/2007/jun/in-no-time#.Uo-ZEKX2tdR.

Also see: Brian Greene, "A Physicist Explains Why Time May Not Exist," NPR Books (January 24, 2011)
website: http://www.npr.org/2011/01/24/132932268/
a-physicist-explains-why-parallel-universes-may-exist.
Also see Andrew Zimmerman Jones and Daniel Robbins, "The Theory of Parallel Universes," For Dummies website (accessed 2013): http://www.dummies.com/how-to/content/
the-theory-of-parallel-universes.html.

3. Some physicists theorize that time doesn't exist at all. See Carlo Rovelli, *Quantum Gravity* (New York: Cambridge University Press, 2007). In 1993, in collaboration with Alain Connes, Rovelli has proposed the thermal time hypothesis. According to this hypothesis, time emerges only in a thermodynamic or statistical context. If this is correct, the flow of time is an illusion, one deriving from the incompleteness of knowledge.

CHAPTER ONE: YOU ARE GREATER

Epigraph. Nikola Tesla. Website:
http://www.goodreads.com/quotes/139502-the-day-science-begins-to-study-
non-physical-phenomena-it-will.

1. Albert Einstein, as quoted in an article, "Atomic Education Urged by Einstein," New York Times (May 25, 1946).

2. According to UCLA professor Ian Bindloss, "Contributions of Physics to the Information Age" (2003) http://www.physics.ucla.edu/~ianb/history, in 1929, physicist Paul Dirac said that "all of chemistry could, in principle, be explained in terms of the newly formulated theory of quantum physics," as the structure of every atom in the universe is determined by quantum mechanics. An understanding of quantum mechanics is necessary to engineer solid-state devices such as transistors that are the building blocks of electronics and computers. Quantum electrodynamics is the physics of lasers and the interaction of light with matter. The laser is used in fiber optics, which are the basis for the huge global telecommunications industry. Even the light entering your eye from a computer screen requires quantum mechanics to understand. Without quantum mechanics, the information age and much of modern science would not exist today.

CHAPTER TWO: YOUR NATURAL ABILITIES

Epigraph. Arthur C. Clarke. Dubbed Clarke's "Second Law" by his readers, this comment appeared in "Hazards of Prophecy: The Failure of Imagination" in the collection *Profiles of the Future: An Inquiry into the Limits of the Possible* (London: Gollancz, 1962).

1. Ibid.

2. Jan Hilgevoord, "The Uncertainty Principle," *Stanford Encyclopedia of Philosophy* website (posted October 8, 2001, revised July 3, 2006): http://plato.stanford.edu/archives/sum2012/entries/qt-uncertainty.

CHAPTER THREE: CREATING FROM ENERGY

Epigraph. Jane Roberts, *Seth Speaks: The Eternal Validity of the Soul* (San Rafael, CA.: Amber-Allen Publishing, 1972): p. 6.

1. International Association on New Science. Founded in 1990, the purpose of this now-defunct association was to bring together scientists, professionals, and lay people to promote research and education in the areas of new science. It was dedicated to research in the education of both traditional and not-traditional fields of science. Founders included scientist and former NASA astronaut, Brian O'Leary. I was a frequent speaker at IANS.

2. Anita Moorjani, *Dying to Be Me* (Carlsbad, CA.: Hay House, 2012). Anita was a guest on my show on July 23, 2012 and November 19, 2012. Listen to her archived interviews: http://www.lifecolorscity.com/en/shows/archives.

3. Placebo and nocebo definitions. See "Putting the Placebo Effect to Work," Harvard Health Publications website (April 2012): http://www.health.harvard.edu/newsletters/Harvard_Health_Letter/2012/April/putting-the-placebo-effect-to-work. Also see "The Nocebo Response," *Harvard Health Publications* website http://www.health.harvard.edu/newsweek/The_nocebo_response.htm and "Understanding the Nocebo Effect," *Harvard Health Publications* website: http://www.health.harvard.edu/press_releases/understanding-the-nocebo-effect.

4. Bruce H. Lipton, *The Biology of Belief* (Carlsbad, CA.: Hay House, 2008): p. xv. Also see Bruce Lipton, "The Wisdom of Your Cells" (posted June 2012): www.brucelipton.com/media/wisdom-your-cells.

5. William J. Cromie, "Meditation Changes Temperatures: Mind Controls Body in Extreme Experiments," *Harvard University Gazette* website (posted April 2002): http://news.harvard.edu/gazette/2002/04.18/09-tummo.html.

6. Robert Lanza, "Five Reasons You Won't Die," *Huffington Post* website (posted January 20, 2011): http://www.huffingtonpost.com/robert-lanza/5-reasons-you-wont-die_b_810936.html.
Also see: Robert Lanza and Bob Berman, *Biocentrism: How Life and Consciousness are the Keys to Understanding the True Nature of the Universe* (Dallas, TX.: BenBella Books, 2013). Also see: Albert Einstein: http://www.goodreads.com/quotes/4455-energy-cannot-be-created-or-destroyed-it-can-only-be.

7. Neurons described.
http://www.brainfacts.org/Brain-Basics/Neuroanatomy/Articles/2012/The-Neuron.

8. "What are Brainwaves," Transparent Corporation website (accessed November 2013): http://www.transparentcorp.com/products/np/brainwaves.php.
Also see Ned Herrmann, "What Is the Function of the Various Brainwaves?" *Scientific American* website (accessed November 2013): http://www.scientificamerican.com/article.cfm?id=what-is-the-function-of-t-1997-12-22.

9. From a book review by Len Wisneski and Lucy Anderson, "The Scientific Basis of Integrative Medicine," *Evidence-based Complementary and Alternative Medicine,* vol. 2, no. 2 (June 2005): pp. 257–259. Website: http://www.ncbi.nlm.nih.gov/pmc/articles/PMC1142191.

10. With the ability to see auras and energy fields, I have witnessed this energy affect the aura and then extend out beyond the aura. Other people, especially healers, have reported to me that they are also able to sense the energy radiating from others.

11. John S. Hagelin, Maxwell V. Rainforth, David W. Orme-Johnson, et al., "Effects of Group Practice of the Transcendental Meditation Program on Preventing Violent Crime in Washington, DC: Results of the National Demonstration Project, June–July 1993," *Social Indicators Research,* vol. 47, no 2 (June 1999): pp. 153–201. Also available on the website: http://istpp.org/crime_prevention.

12. Ibid.

13. The holographic principle was originally developed in 1994 by Dutch Nobel laureate Gerard 't Hooft, and shortly thereafter by Stanford physicist Leonard Susskind. See L. Susskind, "The World as a Hologram," *Journal of Mathematical Physics,* vol. 36, no. 11 (November 1995): pp. 6377–96. Also

see Raphael Bousso, "The Holographic Principle," *Review of Modern Physics,* vol. 74, no. 3: p. 825. In Brian Greene's 2011 book *The Hidden Reality: Parallel Universes and the Deep Laws of the Cosmos* (New York: Vintage, 2011), he suggests a tightly-interlocked holographic multiverse. See Michael Talbot, *The Holographic Universe: The Revolutionary Theory of Reality* (New York: Harper Perennial, 2011). Also see Vienna University of Technology, "How Many Dimensions in the Holographic Universe?" *ScienceDaily* (February 9, 2009). Website: http://www.sciencedaily.com/releases/2009/02/090203081609.htm.

14. Andrew Zimmerman Jones, "Niels Bohr Quotes," *About.com.* Website: http://physics.about.com/od/nielsbohr/tp/Niels-Bohr-Quotes.htm.

15. "Notable Quotes on Quantum Physics," *Quantum Enigma* (accessed November 2013). Website: http://quantumenigma.com/nutshell/notable-quotes-on-quantum-physics.

16. National Aeronautics and Space Administration, "Dark Energy, Dark Matter," *NASA.gov* (accessed November 2013): http://science.nasa.gov/astrophysics/focus-areas/what-is-dark-energy. Also see Goddard Space Flight Center, "Ask an Astrophysicist: What is the difference between Dark Energy and Dark Matter?" (posted January 4, 2001). Website: http://imagine.gsfc.nasa.gov/docs/ask_astro/answers/010104a.html.

17. Erwin Schrödinger, *What Is Life? With Mind and Matter and Autobiographical Sketches* (New York: Cambridge University Press, 2012). Also see Science Joy Wagon, "The Cloud Model" (accessed November 2013): http://www.regentsprep.org/regents/physics/phys05/catomodel/cloud.htm; *Atomic Theory,* "Lesson 1–Page 7" (accessed November 2013): http://www.msnucleus.org/membership/html/jh/physical/atomictheory/lesson1/atomic1g.html; John Carl Villanueva, "Electron Cloud Model," *UniverseToday* (posted August 25, 2009): http://www.universetoday.com/38282/electron-cloud-model; and ABCTE, "Modern Atomic Theory: Models" (accessed November 2013): http://www.abcte.org/files/previews/chemistry/s1_p6.html; and the video: "Dr. Quantum: Wave particle duality and the observer," *YouTube* (posted March 12, 2011): http://www.youtube.com/watch?v=zKdoElvX7k4. Also see "Young Two-slit Experiment" (accessed November 2013): http://abyss.uoregon.edu/~js/21st_century_science/lectures/lec13.html.

18. Stephen Reucroft, "What Exactly is the Higgs Boson? Have Physicists Proved That It Really Exists?" *Scientific American* (posted October 21, 1999). Website: http://www.scientificamerican.com/article.cfm?id=what-exactly-is-the-higgs.

Also see Dave Goldberg, physicist, "What's the Matter with the Higgs Boson?" io9 (posted November 17, 2010). Website: http://io9.com/5690248/whats-the-matter-with-the-higgs-boson. And see Alok Jha, "One Year on from the Higgs Boson Find, Has Physics Hit the Buffers?" *Guardian* (posted August 6, 2013). Website: http://www.theguardian.com/science/2013/aug/06/higgs-boson-physics-hits-buffers-discovery. And see Adam Mann, "Higgs Boson Gets Nobel Prize, But Physicists Still Don't Know What It Means," *Wired* (posted October 8, 2013). Website: http://www.wired.com/wiredscience/2013/10/higgs-nobel-physics.

19. Brian Greene, *The Elegant Universe: Superstrings, Hidden Dimensions, and the Quest for The Ultimate Theory* (New York: W. W. Norton & Company, 2010). Also see Alberto Güijosa, "What Is String Theory?" (accessed November 2013): http://www.nuclecu.unam.mx/~alberto/physics/string.html.

20. David Deutsch, *The Beginning of Infinity: Explanations That Transform the World* (New York: Penguin Books, 2012).

21. Peter Russell, "No Matter." Spirit of Now website: http://www.peterrussell.com/Reality/RHTML/R21.php.

22. See Andrew Zimmerman Jones. Also see Jaime Trosper, "Know Your Scientist—Niels Bohr: The Father of the Atom," *From Quarks to Quasars* (posted September 29, 2013). Website: http://www.fromquarkstoquasars.com/know-your-scientist-niels-bohr-the-father-of-the-atom.

23. National Aeronautics and Space Administration.

24. Video, "The Secret Beyond Matter: 'The External World' Inside Our Brain (Harun Yahya)," *YouTube*: http://www.youtube.com/watch?v=cEDIl7pqTYo. Also see "George Berkeley," Great Philosophers (accessed November 2013). Website: http://oregonstate.edu/instruct/phl201/modules/Philosophers/Berkeley/berkeley.html.

25. Matt Rosenberg, "How Fast Does the Earth Spin?" *About.com* Geography: http://geography.about.com/library/faq/blqzearthspin.htm.

26. C. Monroe, D.M. Meekhof, B.E. King, and D.J. Wineland, "A 'Schrödinger Cat' Superposition State of an Atom," *National Institute of Standards and Technology* (accessed November 2013). Website: http://citeseerx.ist.psu.edu/viewdoc/download?doi=10.1.1.51.1550&rep=rep1&type=pdf. Also see *Wikipedia*, "Quantum Superposition" (accessed November 2013). Website: http://www.princeton.edu/~achaney/tmve/wiki100k/docs/

Quantum_superposition.html.

27. *Wikipedia,* "Science Reference: Schrodinger's Cat," *ScienceDaily* (accessed November 2013). Website:
http://www.sciencedaily.com/articles/s/schrodinger's_cat.htm.
Also see Melody Kramer, "The Physics Behind Schrödinger's Cat Paradox," National Geographic (August 12, 2013). Website:
http://news.nationalgeographic.com/news/2013/08/
130812-physics-schrodinger-erwin-google-doodle-cat-paradox-science.

28. Jan Faye, "Copenhagen Interpretation of Quantum Mechanics," *Stanford Encyclopedia of Philosophy* (accessed November 2013). Website:
http://plato.stanford.edu/entries/qm-copenhagen.
Also see Ben Best, "The Copenhagen Interpretation of Quantum Mechanics," Ben Best website: http://www.benbest.com/science/quantum.html.

29. "Erwin Schrödinger Quotable Quote," *Goodreads* (accessed November 2013). Website: https://www.goodreads.com/quotes/325387-consciousness-cannot-be-accounted-for-in-physical-terms-for-consciousness.
Also see Erwin Schrödinger, *My View of the World* (New York: Cambridge University Press, 1964).

30. Jos Uffink, "The Uncertainty Principle," *Stanford Encyclopedia of Philosophy* (posted October 8, 2001, revised July 3, 2006). Website:
http://plato.stanford.edu/entries/qt-uncertainty. Also see Werner Heisenberg, *Encounters with Einstein: And Other Essays on people, Places, and Particles* (Princeton, N.J.: Princeton University Press, 1989).

31. "Definition of Idealism," *Philosophy-Dictionary.org* (accessed November 2013). Website:
http://www.philosophy-dictionary.org/Kant-Dictionary/BERKELEY/Bohr/
Heisenberg/Idealism.
Also see Werner Heisenberg, *The Physical Principles of the Quantum Theory* (New York: Dover Publications, 1949) and Werner Heisenberg, "Nobel Lecture: The Development of Quantum Mechanics," *Nobelprize.org* (December 11, 1933). Website:
http://www.nobelprize.org/nobel_prizes/physics/laureates/1932/
heisenberg-lecture.html.

32. Erwin Schrödinger, *Mind and Matter* (New York: Cambridge University Press, 1958).

33. William A. Tiller, "How the Power of Intention Alters Matter," *SpiritofMaat.com* (accessed November 2013). Website:
http://www.spiritofmaat.com/archive/mar2/tiller.htm.

34. Jill Bolte-Taylor, *My Stroke of Insight* (New York: Viking, 2008). Also watch the video of Bolte-Taylor's TED Talk: http://www.youtube.com/watch?v=UyyjU8fzEYU.

35. "If ye have faith as a grain of mustard seed, ye shall say unto this mountain, Remove hence to yonder place; and it shall remove; and nothing shall be impossible unto you," Matthew 17:20, *Bible,* King James version. Also see Mark 11:23: "For verily I say unto you, That whosoever shall say unto this mountain, Be thou removed, and be thou cast into the sea; and shall not doubt in his heart, but shall believe that those things which he saith shall come to pass; he shall have whatsoever he saith," Mark 11:24: "Therefore I say unto you, What things soever ye desire, when ye pray, believe that ye receive them, and ye shall have them," and Mark 9:23: "Jesus said unto him, If thou canst believe, all things are possible to him that believeth."

CHAPTER FOUR:
INTUITION, TELEPATHY, AND PSYCHIC ABILITIES

Epigraph. Dalai Lama, "Ethics of Altruism: Lesson 13: An Ethic of Peace," *Dalai Lama Foundation.* Website: http://learning.dalailamafoundation.org/101/ethics13b.htm.

1. "Scientific Foundation: The Unified Field," *Invincibility.org* (accessed November 2013). Website: http://www.invincibility.org/uf_consciousness.html.
   Also see the video: John Hagelin, "Is Consciousness the Unified Field? A Field Theorist's Perspective," *YouTube* (posted December 14, 2011): http://www.youtube.com/watch?v=Fqdcdky9wR4.
   A number of physicists and others share information on the field of consciousness in *Journal of Consciousness Studies.* Of particular interest is Johnjoe McFadden, "Synchronous Firing and Its Influence on the Brain's Electromagnetic Field: Evidence for an Electromagnetic Field Theory of Consciousness," *Journal of Consciousness Studies* (accessed November 2013). Website: http://www.imprint.co.uk/editor.htm.

2. *Star Wars,* script and direction by George Lucas (1977).

3. Maryann Mott, "Did Animals Sense the Tsunami Was Coming?" *National Geographic News* (January 4, 2005). Website: http://news.nationalgeographic.com/news/2005/01/0104_050104_ tsunami_animals.html.

Also watch the video "How Did Animals in Thailand Know the Tsunami Was Coming?" *FirstScienceTV* (uploaded October 22, 2007). Website: http://youtu.be/G8Fy8CNu11U.

4. This quote is found in Albert Einstein's Letter to Morris Raphael Cohen, Professor Emeritus of Philosophy at the College of the City of New York, defending the appointment of Bertrand Russell to a teaching position (March 19, 1940).

5. Jane Roberts, *The Nature of Personal Reality* (San Rafael, CA.: Amber-Allen Publishing, 1994).

6. Biography of Isaac Newton. *Wolfram Research* website: http://scienceworld.wolfram.com/biography/Newton.html.

7. Jeffrey Bub, "Quantum Entanglement and Information," *Stanford Encyclopedia of Philosophy* (Winter 2010 Edition), Edward N. Zalta (ed.). Website: http://plato.stanford.edu/entries/qt-entangle.
Also see Andrew Zimmerman Jones, "What Is Quantum Entanglement?" *About.com* (accessed December 3, 2013). Website: http://physics.about.com/od/quantumphysics/f/QuantumEntanglement.htm.
And see Andrew Zimmerman Jones, "What Is Bell's Theorem?" *About.com* (accessed December 3, 2013). Website: http://physics.about.com/od/quantuminterpretations/f/bellstheorem.htm

8. Josh Clark, "How Quantum Suicide Works," *How Stuff Works* website (accessed December 3, 2013): http://science.howstuffworks.com/innovation/science-questions/quantum-suicide2.htm.

9. Erwin Schrödinger, "Discussion of Probability Relations between Separated Systems," *Mathematical Proceedings of the Cambridge Philosophical Society*, vol. 31, no. 4 (October 1935): pp 555–63. Website: http://dx.doi.org/10.1017/S0305004100013554.

10. Global Consciousness Project. http://noosphere.princeton.edu.
"The Global Consciousness Project" is an international effort involving researchers from several institutions and countries, designed to explore whether the construct of interconnected consciousness can be scientifically validated through objective measurement. The project builds on excellent experiments conducted over the past 35 years at a number of laboratories, demonstrating that human consciousness interacts with random event generators, apparently 'causing' them to produce non-random patterns."

11. Fritjof Capra, *The Tao of Physics: An Exploration of the Parallels Between Modern Physics and Eastern Mysticism* (Boston, MA.: Shambhala, 1975).

12. Richard Bach, *Illusions: The Adventures of a Reluctant Messiah* (Arrow Books, 2001).

CHAPTER FIVE: ENERGY FIELDS AND AURAS

Epigraph. True origin unknown. Often attributed to philosopher Arthur Schopenhauer. *The Harper Book of Quotations*, 3rd edition: p. 451. Website: https://cs.uwaterloo.ca/~shallit/Papers/stages.pdf.

1. Semyon Kirlian (1898–1978) was a Russian inventor and researcher who, along with his wife, invented Kirlian photography. Semyon Kirlian and Valentina Kirlian, "Photography and Visual Observation by Means of High-Frequency Currents," *Journal of Scientific and Applied Photography*, vol. 6, no. 6 (1963). To learn about the history of Kirlian photography, go to the British Institute of Kirlian Photography website: http://kirlianphotography.webs.com/history.htm. Regarding gas discharge visualization (GDV) cameras, see: Konstantin Korotkov, "What is EPI/GDV Bio-electography?" GDV USA website: http://gdvusa.org.
Also see Dr. Korotkov's Lab website:
http://korotkov.org/epcgdv-camera-by-dr-korotkov;
and watch a video: "About GDV Camera (Kirlian Effect) by Prof. Korotkov," *YouTube.com* (posted October 6, 2011):
http://www.youtube.com/watch?v=vuLb5_qPjIM.

2. An electroencephalogram (EEG) is a test that measures and records the electrical activity of your brain. Read more on *WebMD*:
http://www.webmd.com/epilepsy/electroencephalogram-eeg-21508.
An electrocardiogram (EKG or ECG) is a test that checks for problems with the electrical activity of your heart. Read more about it on *WebMD*:
http://www.webmd.com/heart-disease/electrocardiogram.

3. From 2003–2007, National Institutes of Health funded research on human biofields through the Laboratory for Advances in Consciousness and Health (LACH). Website:
http://lach.web.arizona.edu/center_frontier_medicine_biofield_science_cfmbs.
Also see S.L. Warber, D. Cornelio, J. Straughn, and G. Kile, "Biofield Energy Healing from the Inside," *Journal of Alternative and Complementary Medicine*, vol. 10, no. 6 (December 2004): pp. 1107–13. You can read an abstract:

http://www.ncbi.nlm.nih.gov/pubmed/15674009.

4. Beverly Rubik, *Institute for Frontier Science,* PMB 605, 6114 LaSalle Avenue, Oakland, CA. 94611. Read Daniel Redwood's interview with Rubik, "Frontier Science," at *Healthy.net:* www.healthy.net/scr/interview.aspx?Id=220. Also see her biography on the Ions Directory: http://noetic.org/directory/person/beverly-rubik.

5. Learn more about Gary Schwartz, director of the Laboratory for Advances in Consciousness and Health at the University of Arizona, at: http://lach.web.arizona.edu/lab_members and http://www.drgaryschwartz.com.

Chapter Six: Parallel Universes

Epigraph. Richard Bach, *Jonathan Livingston Seagull* (New York: Scribner, 2006).

1. Hugh Everett devised the many worlds theory and coined the term multiverse. To learn more, see Peter Byrne, "The Many Worlds of Hugh Everett," *Scientific American* (October 21, 2008). Website: www.scientificamerican.com/article.cfm?id=hugh-everett-biography. Also see the transcript of the NOVA episode hosted by Mark Everett, "Parallel Worlds, Parallel Lives," which aired on *PBS* on October 21, 2008. Website: http://www-tc.pbs.org/wgbh/nova/manyworlds; and Vmdamico, "Parallel Universes Really Do Exist," Environmental Graffiti. Website: www.environmentalgraffiti.com/physics/news-parallel-universes-proven-physics.

2. David Deutsch, as quoted by Tim Folger and Morgane Le Gall, "Physics' Best Kept Secret," *Discover,* vol. 22, no. 9 (September 1, 2001): p. 36. Read online: http://discovermagazine.com/2001/sep/cover#.UnL2DBb2tdQ. Also see: http://daviddeutsch.physics.ox.ac.uk/index.php?path=Parallel%20Universes and http://daviddeutsch.physics.ox.ac.uk/David.html.

3. Ibid.

4. Ibid.

5. Psalm 37:11, *Bible,* King James version.

6. Jane Roberts, *Seth Speaks: The Eternal Validity of the Soul* (San Rafael, CA.: Amber-Allen Publishing, 1994).

7. Read the full text of the Declaration of Independence: http://www.archives.gov/exhibits/charters/declaration_transcript.html.

8. Tim Folger and Morgane Le Gall.

9. Craig Rosen, "The Origins of Some of Paul McCartney's Greatest Songs," *Yahoo! Music* (posted October 11, 2013). Website: http://music.yahoo.com/blogs/stop-the-presses/origins-paul-mccartney-greatest-songs-160242483.html.

10. In 1801, Thomas Young presented a famous paper to the Royal Society entitled "On the Theory of Light and Colours," which described various interference phenomena, and in 1803 he performed his famous double-slit experiment. Thomas Young , "The Bakerian Lecture: On the Theory of Light and Colours," *Philosophical Transactions of the Royal Society of London,* vol. 92 (1802): pp. 12–48. Website: http://www.jstor.org/stable/107113. Also watch the video "Thomas Young's Double Slit Experiment," MITVideo website: http://video.mit.edu/watch/thomas-youngs-double-slit-experiment-8432. And see Bryan Clintberg, "Lesson 58: Young's Double Slit Experiment," *Mr. Clintberg's Study Physics!* Website: http://www.studyphysics.ca/newnotes/20/unit04_light/chp1719_light/lesson58.htm.

11. Peter Byrne, speaking about Hugh Everett during an interview conducted on August 29, 2008, and edited by Peter Tyson, editor in chief of *NOVA Online.* "The Many Worlds Theory Today," *NOVA* (posted October 21, 2008). Read on the PBS website: http://www.pbs.org/wgbh/nova/physics/many-worlds-theory-today.html.

12. Ibid.

13. Tim Folger and Morgane Le Gall.

14. Ibid.

CHAPTER SEVEN; OTHER LIVES

Epigraph. Erwin Schrodinger. *Brainyquote.com*

1. Brian Weiss, *Many Lives, Many Masters: The True Story of a Prominent Psychiatrist, His Young Patient, and the Past-Life Therapy That Changed Both Their Lives* (New York: Fireside, 1988).

2. Jenny Cockell, *Journeys Through Time* (London, UK.: Piatkus Press, 2010). Also see Jenny Cockell, *Yesterday's Children: The Search for My Family from the Past* (London, UK.: Piatkus Books, 1993). And watch the videos: Jacqueline Radley (producer), UK Living, "A Life Revisited," www.youtube.com/watch?v=M6yl75kfhqM; and Bob Olson, "Past Life Memories Lead Woman to Reunite with Her Children from Previous Lifetime," *AfterlifeTV*: www.afterlifetv.com/?p 1582.

3. Cameron Macaulay was featured in the documentary "Extraordinary People: The Boy Who Lived Before," *Channel 5 Broadcasting Ltd.* Watch on YouTube (posted June 2011): http://www.youtube.com/watch?v 2WhOOsVtdeE.

4. Ian Stevenson wrote two books on the subject of children and reincarnation. *Twenty Cases Suggestive of Reincarnation,* second edition, revised and enlarged (Charlottesville, VA.: University of Virginia Press, 1980); and *Children Who Remember Previous Lives: A Question of Reincarnation,* revised edition (Jefferson, N.C.: McFarland & Company, 2000).

5. Ian Stevenson, *Twenty Cases Suggestive of Reincarnation:* p. 9.

6. Ibid: p. 357.

7. Ibid: p. 20

8. Ibid: p. 325

9. Matthew 17:10–13, *Bible,* King James version.

CHAPTER EIGHT: TALKING TO THE OTHER SIDE

Epigraph. Jane Roberts, *Seth Speaks: The Eternal Validity of the Soul* (San Rafael, CA.: Amber-Allen Publishing, 1972): p. 41.

1. Eben Alexander, *Proof of Heaven: A Neurosurgeon's Journey into the Afterlife* (New York: Simon & Schuster, 2012).

CHAPTER NINE: EXPLORING FURTHER

Epigraph. Arthur C. Clarke, *Profiles of the Future: An Inquiry into the Limits of the Possible,* revised edition (New York: Henry Holt & Co, 1984). Clarke's Third Law: Any sufficiently advanced technology is indistinguishable from magic.

CONCLUSION

Epigraph. John 10:34, *Bible,* King James version.

ABOUT THE AUTHOR

Pamala Oslie is a professional psychic, author, consultant, and radio show host, who has the ability to see auras. She has appeared on numerous national television and radio shows, been a featured speaker at the 2012 TEDx Talks, and presented to Fortune 500 companies and at different conferences on science and consciousness. Since 1984, Pamala has spoken about the emerging human potential, psychic abilities, auras, quantum physics, and the power of our beliefs to create our reality. Pamala has written many popular books and has an extensive international clientele. She lives in Santa Barbara, California.

To contact Pamala, please write to:

Pamala Oslie
P.O. Box 30035
Santa Barbara, CA. 93130
1 (805) 687-6604

You can learn more about her at: http://www.lifecolorscity.com.